2015 Revision
of CSET Math I
Study Guide:
Number and Quantity; Algebra

Copyright 2015 by Christopher Goff

University of the Pacific

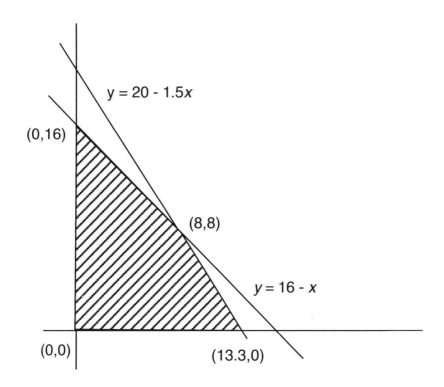

Domains Covered:

1.1 The Real and Complex Number Systems

a. Demonstrate knowledge of the properties of the real number system and of its subsets

1. What are the real numbers?

   On a superficial level, each real number corresponds to a point on the number line, and vice versa. The real numbers include not only the whole numbers and ratios of whole numbers, but also all the numbers in between, including the "irrational" numbers.

   On a deeper level, the question of the nature of the real numbers is really more philosophical, getting at the very notion of number itself. In some textbooks, the real numbers are assumed to exist as a starting point of the discussion. This means there is no need to deduce their existence mathematically; it is just assumed by fiat. Other books construct the real numbers from the rational numbers. (We will define the rational numbers below.) The German mathematician Richard Dedekind (1831-1916) defined a real number in terms of two sets of rational numbers, all those less than or equal to the real number, and all those greater than it. (This is known as a Dedekind "cut.") We will choose the informal approach with which we began, namely, that the real numbers are in one-to-one correspondence with the points on the number line.

2. What are some properties of the real numbers?

   Many properties of the real numbers come from the fact that the set of all real numbers is a field. For a list of field properties, see below in section **2.1 Algebraic Structures**, part **a.** For now, we will just state that the real numbers are closed under addition and multiplication, each of which is commutative and associative. Also, addition and multiplication have their respective identity elements, and each element has an additive inverse. Every element except zero has a multiplicative inverse. Multiplication distributes over addition.

   There are also properties involving ordering, such as "greater than". See section **2.1.b** for more information about ordering properties.

   Finally, what sets the real numbers apart from the rational numbers (defined below) is the idea of "completeness". Sometimes it is phrased that any convergent sequence of rational numbers has to converge to a real number. But a more common way to say it is that any set of real numbers that is bounded above has a least upper bound that is itself a real number.

   For instance, consider the interval $[0, 1)$. This is the set of all real numbers that are greater than or equal to 0 and less than 1. The numbers 1, 1.5, 2, $\pi/2$, and e are upper bounds for this interval (and there are many more upper bounds). But of all the upper bounds, there is a least one, that is, one that is smaller than all the others. In this case, that is the number 1. Notice that 1 is not part of the interval in question, but it is the smallest upper bound for that interval.

   To see why this property is not shared by the rational numbers, see the Sample Problems.

3. What are some of the subsets of real numbers?

   Let's begin with what many would call the first infinite set: the natural numbers. Also called the counting numbers, the natural numbers contain 1, 2, 3, 4, etc. One can describe the natural numbers by saying that they contain the number 1, and that for every natural number n, the number $n+1$ is also a natural number. The number 0 is not considered natural (in most mathematics textbooks), nor is -2, for instance.

Some books list the whole numbers as a separate set from the natural numbers. For these books, the whole numbers begin at 0 and continue upward to 1, 2, 3, etc. (Some books call *this* set the natural numbers. Check your textbook to be sure.) Numbers like -2 and -5 are not considered whole numbers.

Next come the integers, which are basically the smallest set to contain the natural numbers as well as each natural number's additive inverse, as well as zero. So the integers contain $0, 1, -1, 2, -2, 3, -3$, etc. Numbers like 2.5 and π are not integers.

The next important set is the rational numbers, which can be described as all the ratios of two integers, provided that you do not divide by zero. In other words, every rational number can be written as $\frac{p}{q}$, where p and q are integers, and $q \neq 0$. Moreover, every number that can be written in this form is rational. Some examples of rational numbers are: $\frac{22}{7}, \frac{1}{4}, -\frac{2}{23}, -5, 0,$ and $\frac{22349}{34}$. Some numbers that are not rational are $\sqrt{2}, \pi$, and e.

4. What properties differ among the subsets of the real numbers?

   The following table compiles key properties. All the sets described so far are closed under addition and multiplication, are ordered by $<$, and each contains 1, the multiplicative identity.

Number set	Additive identity in set	Additive inverses in set	Multiplicative inverses in set	Complete
Natural numbers	No	No	No	No
Whole numbers	Yes	No	No	No
Integers	Yes	Yes	No	No
Rational numbers	Yes	Yes	Yes	No
Real numbers	Yes	Yes	Yes	Yes

5. Sample Problems

   (a) Why aren't the rational numbers "complete"?

   (b) True or false. Explain your answers.

       i. The set of even integers is closed under addition.
       ii. The set of even integers is closed under multiplication.
       iii. The set of odd integers is closed under addition.
       iv. The set of odd integers is closed under multiplication.

6. Answers to Sample Problems

   (a) Why aren't the rational numbers "complete"?

       The main reason that the rational numbers are not complete is that there are sets that are bounded above, but do not have a smallest rational number as a least upper bound.

For instance, consider the set of all rational numbers less than $\sqrt{2}$. Clearly, $\sqrt{2}$ is an upper bound for this set (as is 2, 3, 4, etc.). But $\sqrt{2} \approx 1.414\ldots$ is not a rational number. (Euclid gave a proof of this fact in his *Elements* c. 300 BCE.) Let's suppose that we choose 1.415 as an upper bound. Since $1.415 = \frac{1415}{1000} = \frac{283}{200}$, then 1.415 is rational. And since $1.415^2 = 2.002225 > 2$, we know by taking square roots that $1.415 > \sqrt{2}$. So yes, 1.415 really is an upper bound for the set of rational numbers that are smaller than $\sqrt{2}$. But is it the least upper bound? The answer is no. There is another rational number, 1.4143 that is smaller than 1.415 but still larger than $\sqrt{2}$, because $1.4143^2 = 2.00024449 > 2$. Is 1.4143 the least upper bound? The answer is again no because we can go to the next decimal place and choose an upper bound there: 1.41422 is smaller than 1.4143, but is still larger than $\sqrt{2}$. Dedekind explained that there is always another rational number between $\sqrt{2}$ and any rational number greater than $\sqrt{2}$, and he found a formula for how to find it. I will let you look up Dedekind's work if you wish (or figure it out for yourself), but I hope that the consideration of subsequent decimal places will at least convince you that there is no way to find a smallest rational number that is greater than $\sqrt{2}$. (We used $\sqrt{2}$ here as an example, as did Dedekind, but of course any other irrational number would prove the same point.)

(b) True or false. Explain your answers.

   i. The set of even integers is closed under addition. [True.]

      Even integers can be written as $2k$, where k is an integer. So if you had two of them, say $2k$ and 2ℓ, then their sum would be $2k + 2\ell = 2(k + \ell)$. This is again an even integer, because it is twice the integer $k + \ell$. (We know $k + \ell$ is an integer because k and ℓ are each integers, and we know that the set of integers is closed under addition - see the chart above.) Hence the set of even integers is closed under addition.

   ii. The set of even integers is closed under multiplication. [True.]

      As before, choose $2k$ and 2ℓ as our even integers, where k and l are integers. Then their product, $(2k)(2\ell) = 4k\ell = 2(2k\ell)$, is again an even integer because it is twice the integer $2k\ell$. How do we know $2k\ell$ is an integer? We know because $2, k$, and ℓ are integers and the set of integers is closed under multiplication. Hence the set of even integers is also closed under multiplication.

   iii. The set of odd integers is closed under addition. [False.]

      The set of odd integers is not closed under addition. We could prove that the sum of two odd integers is even, but the way the question is asked, we only need to provide a single counterexample to disprove the statement. In other words, we only need to find two odd numbers whose sum is not odd. So consider the numbers 3 and 5. $3 + 5 = 8 = 2(4)$. Since 8 is even (being twice the integer 4), it is not odd. Therefore the set of odd integers is not closed under addition.

   iv. The set of odd integers is closed under multiplication. [True.]

      Unlike even numbers, odd numbers have the form $2k + 1$, where k is an integer. So let us pick two odd integers, $2k + 1$ and $2\ell + 1$, where k and ℓ are integers. Then the product is

$$(2k + 1)(2\ell + 1) = 4k\ell + 2k + 2\ell + 1 = 2(2k\ell + k + \ell) + 1,$$

which is again in the form $2m + 1$, where m is the integer $2k\ell + k + \ell$. How do we know m is an integer? We know because $2, k$ and ℓ are integers and we know that the set of integers is closed under addition and multiplication. Therefore the set of odd integers is closed under multiplication.

b. Perform operations and recognize equivalent expressions using various representations of real numbers (e.g., fractions, decimals, exponents)

1. What is the difference between fractions, decimals, and exponents?

   This is perhaps not the most precise language we could use. Instead, we will talk about the difference between rational numbers, decimal representations of numbers, and numbers that are powers.

   We defined rational numbers earlier as the ratio of two integers, provided that the denominator is not zero. In contrast, a decimal representation of a number involves writing it as a sum of powers of 10, including negative powers. As an example, the number 1.5 is a decimal representation of the rational number $\frac{3}{2}$. In its decimal form, we have the following meaning:

   $$1.5 = (1)(10^0) + (5)(10^{-1}) = 1 + \frac{5}{10} = \frac{15}{10} = \frac{3}{2}.$$

   Some numbers are easier to write as rational numbers, like $\frac{1}{3}$. The corresponding decimal representation repeats: $0.333333\ldots$. So while the rational number is easy to write, the decimal representation never terminates. Other numbers may be easier to write as decimals, especially if the numbers are longer, or involve integer parts, like 1032.49975.

   We mentioned powers of 10 earlier. So what is a power, exactly? The term "power" is often defined as a base (usually an integer or rational number) raised to an integer exponent. For example, $2^2 = 4$. We say that 4 is a power of 2. Similarly, 100 is a power of 10, as is $\frac{1}{100}$ (since $10^{-2} = \frac{1}{100}$). Growing up using decimal representations usually makes people pretty comfortable with powers of 10. Computers have made powers of 2 very important as well through their use of binary representations of numbers.

2. How do you add, subtract, multiply, divide, exponentiate, or take roots of real numbers in these representations?

   We will not comprehensively review how to perform operations with rational numbers, decimals, or powers here. Those can be found in any basic arithmetic or algebra text. We will only point out some key properties in each case.

   - Rational Numbers.
     $$\frac{a}{b} + \frac{c}{d} = \frac{ad + bc}{bd} \quad \text{and} \quad \frac{a}{b} \cdot \frac{c}{d} = \frac{ac}{bd}.$$

   - Decimal representations. Addition and multiplication follow the usual integer rules and algorithms. The only difference is that the decimal point needs to be kept track of. For addition, align the decimal points and the add the values as you would for integers, leaving the decimal point in place. For multiplication, the rule of thumb is that the number of digits after the decimal place in the product should equal the sum of the numbers of digits after the decimal place in each factor. You will be asked to explain this rule in the Sample Problems.

- Powers

$$n^a \cdot n^b = n^{a+b} \quad \text{and} \quad (n^a)^b = n^{ab}.$$

Many of the other formulas can be derived from these. See the Sample Problems.

3. How do you convert between equivalent expressions involving real numbers?

We saw a little of this above. To convert from a terminating decimal representation to a rational number, simply write each power of 10 as a fraction, via $10^{-n} = \dfrac{1}{10^n}$. Then add each term using the rules for adding fractions.

To write a repeating decimal as a rational number, there is an algorithm that depends on how many digits repeat. As an example, we will find the rational equivalent of $1.\overline{36}$. Let $x = 1.\overline{36}$. Then $100x = 136.\overline{36}$. Subtracting the former equation from the latter, we get $99x = 135$. So $x = \dfrac{135}{99} = \dfrac{15}{11}$.

To convert a rational number to a decimal, you can use long division. The algorithm is the same as for integers, but keeping track of the decimal point along the way. So the decimal equivalent of $\dfrac{5}{6}$ can be found by dividing $5.000\ldots$ by 6.

$$
\begin{array}{r}
0.833\ldots \\
6 \enclose{longdiv}{5.000\ldots} \\
\underline{48} \\
20 \\
\underline{18} \\
20 \\
\underline{18} \\
2
\end{array}
$$

$\ldots$ and so on. So $\dfrac{5}{6} = 0.8\overline{3}$. In general, you might have to go a long way until the pattern repeats, but a nice property of rational numbers is that their decimal representations always either terminate or eventually repeat (forever).

4. How do you recognize equivalent expressions involving real numbers?

To me, this question is more about experience and having a good memory. I am personally reminded of my sixth-grade math teacher, Mrs. Peters, who made us memorize the squares of the integers from 1 to 25, and the cubes of the integers from 1 to 12. She also made us memorize the decimal equivalents for rational numbers in lowest terms having denominators at most 11. I have lost count as to how many times this knowledge has come in handy. Granted, I became a math professor, but I use the rational-decimal equivalences more in my day-to-day life than in my professional career. Because of my teacher, I can recognize these equivalences when I encounter them in the "real world." Mrs. Peters has inspired me to ask the same of you in the Sample Problems. (She also made us learn the percentage equivalents, but those are so close to the decimal representation that I will skip it here.) (PS - thank you, Mrs. Peters!)

5. Sample Problems

   (a) Using the formula $\frac{a}{b} \cdot \frac{c}{d} = \frac{ac}{bd}$, how can you deduce that that $\frac{1}{\frac{a}{b}} = \frac{b}{a}$ (assuming $a, b \neq 0$)?

   (b) Let $n > 0$. Using the formula $n^a \cdot n^b = n^{a+b}$, how can you deduce that $n^0 = 1$? ...that $n^{-a} = \frac{1}{n^a}$? ...that $n^{1/2} = \sqrt{n}$?

   (c) Why was $1.\overline{36}$ multiplied by 100 in order to find its rational representation?

   (d) Find rational representations for: $0.\overline{4}, 2.\overline{232}$, and $-1.12\overline{3}$.

   (e) Explain why the the number of digits after the decimal place in the product of two decimal representations should equal the sum of the numbers of digits after the decimal place in the decimal representation of each factor.

   (f) (Recognition of powers) List the squares of the numbers from 1 to 25 and the cubes of the numbers from 1 to 12.

   (g) (Recognition of decimal equivalents of rational numbers) List the decimal equivalents of all the rational numbers in lowest terms having denominators at most 11. Notice any patterns?

6. Answers to Sample Problems

   (a) Using the formula $\frac{a}{b} \cdot \frac{c}{d} = \frac{ac}{bd}$, how can you deduce that $\frac{1}{\frac{a}{b}} = \frac{b}{a}$ (assuming $a, b \neq 0$)?

   First, assume $a, b \neq 0$. To answer the questions asked, let's start by answering another question: what is $\frac{a}{b} \cdot \frac{b}{a}$? Well, according to the formula, the product is $\frac{ab}{ab} = 1$. So $\frac{a}{b} \cdot \frac{b}{a} = 1$. If we divide both sides by $\frac{a}{b}$, then we get the desired result.

   (b) Let $n > 0$. Using the formula $n^a \cdot n^b = n^{a+b}$, how can you deduce that $n^0 = 1$? ...that $n^{-a} = \frac{1}{n^a}$? ...that $n^{1/2} = \sqrt{n}$?

   These answers go in order and build on each other. Let's start by considering the formula if $b = 0$, $n \neq 0$. Then $n^a \cdot n^0 = n^{a+0} = n^a$. Dividing both sides by n^a gives the result $n^0 = 1$. For the next result, let $b = -a$ in the formula. Then $n^a \cdot n^{-a} = n^{a+(-a)} = n^0 = 1$. Dividing both sides by n^a gives $n^{-a} = \frac{1}{n^a}$. For the last equation, consider $a = b = \frac{1}{2}$. Then $n^{1/2} \cdot n^{1/2} = n^1 = n$. Since $(n^{1/2})^2 = n$, taking the square root of both sides gives $n^{1/2} = \sqrt{n}$. Notice that this method could be tweaked to show that $n^{1/3} = \sqrt[3]{n}$, etc.

   (c) Why was $1.\overline{36}$ multiplied by 100 in order to find its rational representation?

   The reason is that we need all of the repeated decimals to align in the subtraction, thereby canceling them out. Since it is a two-digit repeating pattern, multiplying by $10^2 = 100$ will align the repeated digits.

(d) Find rational representations for: $0.\overline{4}, 2.\overline{232}$, and $-1.12\overline{3}$.

$$0.\overline{4} = \frac{4}{9}, \quad 2.\overline{232} = \frac{2230}{999} = 2\frac{232}{999}, \quad \text{and} \quad -1.12\overline{3} = -\frac{337}{300} = -1\frac{37}{300}$$

To see the last one, multiply the original by 10. Then subtract the original from this, giving $9x = -10.11$. Since this still has decimals in it, we can multiply both sides by 100, giving $900x = -1011$, or $300x = -337$.

(e) Explain why the the number of digits after the decimal place in the product of two decimal representations should equal the sum of the numbers of digits after the decimal place in the decimal representation of each factor.

Before we give a general reason, let's calculate $0.128 \cdot 0.45$. According to the rule, we should multiply 128 times 45 and then force there to be $3 + 2$, or 5 digits to the right of the decimal in the answer. So, $128 \cdot 45 = 5760$. In order to get this right, we need to count the final zero as one of the digits. So the final answer should be $0.05760 = 0.0576$. You can verify this with a calculator of course.

The question though is why does this algorithm work? Let's look at it another way, after converting each decimal representation to a sum of integers times powers of 10 and then multiplying out all the terms using the distributive property.

$$\begin{aligned} 0.128 \cdot 0.45 &= \left(1 \cdot 10^{-1} + 2 \cdot 10^{-2} + 8 \cdot 10^{-3}\right)\left(4 \cdot 10^{-1} + 5 \cdot 10^{-2}\right) \\ &= 4(10^{-2}) + 5(10^{-3}) + 8(10^{-3}) + 10(10^{-4}) + 32(10^{-4}) + 40(10^{-5}) \\ &= \text{some arithmetic} = 0.0576 \end{aligned}$$

The main point here is to look at the term with the smallest exponent. Here, that term is the 10^{-5} term, which came from the product of the smallest terms of each factor: 10^{-3} times 10^{-2} in this example. Because the exponents add together when multiplying, we get $10^{-3} \cdot 10^{-2} = 10^{-5}$. Notice that the exponent -3 corresponds to three digits to the right of the decimal, and -2 corresponds to two digits. So the -5 corresponds to five digits after the decimal.

In general, the smallest power of 10 in the product will be the product of the smallest powers of 10 in each factor. Since the exponent on the smallest power of 10 corresponds to the number of digits to the right of the decimal, and because the exponents are added when powers of 10 are multiplied, the number of digits to the right of the decimal is additive when multiplying decimal representations together.

(f) (Recognition of powers) List the squares of the numbers from 1 to 25 and the cubes of the numbers from 1 to 12.

x	x^2	x^3	x	x^2
1	1	1	13	169
2	4	8	14	196
3	9	27	15	225
4	16	64	16	256
5	25	125	17	289
6	36	216	18	324
7	49	343	19	361
8	64	512	20	400
9	81	729	21	441
10	100	1000	22	484
11	121	1331	23	529
12	144	1728	24	576
			25	625

(g) (Recognition of decimal equivalents of rational numbers) List the decimal equivalents of all the rational numbers in lowest terms having denominators at most 11. Notice any patterns?

Denominator						
2	$\frac{1}{2} = 0.5$					
3	$\frac{1}{3} = 0.\overline{3}$	$\frac{2}{3} = 0.\overline{6}$				
4	$\frac{1}{4} = 0.25$	$\frac{3}{4} = 0.75$				
5	$\frac{1}{5} = 0.2$	$\frac{2}{5} = 0.4$	$\frac{3}{5} = 0.6$	$\frac{4}{5} = 0.8$		
6	$\frac{1}{6} = 0.1\overline{6}$	$\frac{5}{6} = 0.8\overline{3}$				
7	$\frac{1}{7} = 0.\overline{142857}$	$\frac{2}{7} = 0.\overline{285714}$	$\frac{3}{7} = 0.\overline{428571}$	$\frac{4}{7} = 0.\overline{571428}$	$\frac{5}{7} = 0.\overline{714285}$	$\frac{6}{7} = 0.\overline{857142}$
8	$\frac{1}{8} = 0.125$	$\frac{3}{8} = 0.375$	$\frac{5}{8} = 0.625$	$\frac{7}{8} = 0.875$		
9	$\frac{1}{9} = 0.\overline{1}$	$\frac{2}{9} = 0.\overline{2}$	$\frac{4}{9} = 0.\overline{4}$	$\frac{5}{9} = 0.\overline{5}$	$\frac{7}{9} = 0.\overline{7}$	$\frac{8}{9} = 0.\overline{8}$
10	$\frac{1}{10} = 0.1$	$\frac{3}{10} = 0.3$	$\frac{7}{10} = 0.7$	$\frac{9}{10} = 0.9$		
11 (a)	$\frac{1}{11} = 0.\overline{09}$	$\frac{2}{11} = 0.\overline{18}$	$\frac{3}{11} = 0.\overline{27}$	$\frac{4}{11} = 0.\overline{36}$	$\frac{5}{11} = 0.\overline{45}$	
11 (b)	$\frac{6}{11} = 0.\overline{54}$	$\frac{7}{11} = 0.\overline{63}$	$\frac{8}{11} = 0.\overline{72}$	$\frac{9}{11} = 0.\overline{81}$	$\frac{10}{11} = 0.\overline{90}$	

There are some great patterns here. For the rational numbers with denominator 11, the two repeated digits are the product of 9 and the numerator. For the rational numbers with denominator 7, the digits 1, 4, 2, 8, 5, 7 appear cyclically in the same order. Only the starting number changes. In terms of recognizing decimal equivalents of rational numbers, knowing this table has served me well.

c. Solve real-world and mathematical problems using numerical and algebraic expressions and equations

1. How do you model real-world situations with algebraic expressions, equations, and inequalities?

   Expressions are the nouns in the language of algebra, and equations and inequalities are the sentences. They give us some information about the expressions we are studying. So if we have information about some numbers, then we can translate that information into an equation or inequality.

   As an example, suppose that you bought four children's movie tickets and the cost was $38. We can represent this using expressions and an equation. If we let P represent the price of a child's movie ticket, then the expression representing the cost of four tickets would be $4P$. The equation is therefore $4P = 38$. We will solve this below.

   Now suppose that you don't know exactly what the price of the four children's movie tickets was, but that you did know that it was less than $40. We can represent this as an inequality. Again, if P is the price of one child's ticket, then $4P$ is the price of four children's tickets. The inequality is therefore $4P < 40$. We will solve this below.

2. How do you use equations and inequalities to solve problems?

   We will be working with equations and inequalities that contain variables. That means that there is some unknown quantity in the "sentence." When you solve an equation or inequality, you are finding out the values of the variable(s) that will make the sentence a true statement. So we will create an equation or inequality in such a way that by solving it, we will get the answer we desire.

   In the former example above, we created the equation $4P = 38$. We could solve this equation for P and that would give us the price for one child's movie ticket. We would get $P = 9.5$, or the price of a child's ticket is $9.50. In the latter example, we created the inequality $4P < 40$. If we were to solve this, then it would tell us the maximum price that a single child's ticket could cost. We would get $P < 10$, or the maximum price of a child's ticket is $10. Since the information obtained is slightly different in each case, we want to create the equation or inequality that will lead us to the information we seek.

3. What are some examples?

   See section **2.3.f** for specific examples of linear and non-linear modeling problems.

(d.) **Apply proportional relationships to model and solve real-world and mathematical problems**

1. What is a proportional relationship?

   A quantity A is said to be proportional to another quantity B if there is a constant k satisfying $A = kB$. Often, the quantity B is itself a power of another quantity. For instance, if $B = x^2$, then we can say, "A is proportional to the square of x" or "A is proportional to x^2." I suppose A could also be a power, though in practice that is seldom the case.

2. What is an inversely proportional relationship?

   A quantity A is said to be inversely proportional to another quantity B if there is a constant k satisfying $A = \dfrac{k}{B}$. Often, the quantity B is itself a power of another quantity. For instance, if $B = x^3$, then we can say, "A is inversely proportional to the cube of x" or "A is inversely proportional to x^3." I suppose A could also be a power, though in practice that is seldom the case.

3. What real-world situations can be modeled using proportional relationships?

   Countless real-world situations follow a proportional or inversely proportional relationship. Some proportional examples include: how much you pay for a bunch of bananas, say, is proportional to their weight (or in some stores, to their number); if you drive at a constant speed, the distance traveled is proportional to the time spent driving; the volume of a sphere is proportional to the cube of its radius; the cost of a hotel stay is proportional to the number of nights spent there.

   Some inverse proportionality relationships include: the amount of time it takes to drive somewhere is inversely proportional to the speed at which you drive; the number of bananas you can buy for $3 is inversely proportional to their cost; under constant voltage, the resistance in a circuit is inversely proportional to the current; the amount of each heir's inheritance is inversely proportional to the number of heirs (assuming each heir receives the same amount); the gravitational force between two given stars is inversely proportional to the square of the distance between them.

4. How do you model problems using proportional relationships?

   The key to modeling these problems lies in converting the language of the problem to an equation, namely, the equation that is part of the definition of proportionality. For, example, the volume of a sphere is proportional to the cube of its radius. We can parse this statement like this:

the volume of a sphere	is proportional to	the cube of its radius
V	$= k \cdot$	r^3

   So, $V = kr^3$. Similarly, the amount of each heir's inheritance is inversely proportional to the number of heirs. This can be seen as

the amount of each heir's inheritance	is inversely proportional to	the number of heirs
A	$= k \div$	n

   So, $A = \dfrac{k}{n}$.

5. Sample Problems

   (a) The amount of grass seed needed to cover a square field is proportional to the area of the field. If G represents the amount of grass seed, and x is the length of the square field, write down an equation for this situation. (Use k to represent the constant of proportionality.)

   (b) The volume of a sphere is proportional to the cube of its radius. What happens to the volume if the radius is doubled?

   (c) At Trader Joe's market, the cost of bananas is proportional to the number of bananas you buy. What is the common term for the constant of proportionality in this case? What are its units? If six bananas cost $1.14, the how much would five bananas cost?

(d) Suppose the leader of a family dies, leaving each heir an equal portion of the estate. Suppose each heir is scheduled to receive $300,000. Then another heir is identified and claims an equal share of the estate. With the addition of this new heir, each portion of the estate becomes $250,000. How many original heirs were there? What was the value of the original estate? (Hint: what is the meaning of the constant of proportionality in this case?)

6. Answers to Sample Problems

(a) The amount of grass seed needed to cover a square field is proportional to the area of the field. If G represents the amount of grass seed, and x is the length of the square field, write down an equation for this situation. (Use k to represent the constant of proportionality.) $G = kx^2$.

(b) The volume of a sphere is proportional to the cube of its radius. What happens to the volume if the radius is doubled? The volume is increased by a factor of 8.

To see this, we start with the equation $V = kr^3$ that we determined above. Suppose now that r is doubled to $2r$. Then the new volume, W, satisfies $W = k(2r)^3 = 8kr^3 = 8V$. So W is eight times bigger than V.

(c) At Trader Joe's market, the cost of bananas is proportional to the number of bananas you buy. What is the common term for the constant of proportionality in this case? What are its units? If six bananas cost $1.14, the how much would five bananas cost?

Since cost is proportional to the number bought, our equation becomes $C = kn$. So $k = \dfrac{C}{n}$. In other words, k is just the cost per banana, or the unit cost. (Prices of things are really just constants of proportionality.) At Trader Joe's, the units on k are "cents per banana." To solve the problem, we use the given information to find k, and then we use that information to find the total cost of five bananas. (Note $1.14 = 114$ cents.)

$$
\begin{aligned}
C &= kn \\
114 &= k(6) \\
19 &= k
\end{aligned}
$$

So the cost per banana is 19 cents. We use this to find the cost C for five bananas: $C = (19)(5) = 95$. So five bananas cost 95 cents at Trader Joe's.

(d) Suppose the leader of a family dies, leaving each heir an equal portion of the estate. Suppose each heir is scheduled to receive $300,000. Then another heir is identified and claims an equal share of the estate. With the addition of this new heir, each portion of the estate becomes $250,000. How many original heirs were there? What was the value of the original estate? (Hint: what is the meaning of the constant of proportionality in this case?)

There are two unknowns here: the total amount of the estate and the original number of heirs, n. We haven't really talked about systems of equations yet, but this problem can be solved by substitution as well. We can set up two equations:

$$
300{,}000 = \frac{k}{n} \quad \text{and} \quad 250{,}000 = \frac{k}{n+1}.
$$

Multiplying to clear denominators in each case, we get: $300{,}000n = k$ and $250{,}000(n + 1) = k$. If you analyze this first equation, you see that the amount each original heir was scheduled to receive ($\$300{,}000$) is multiplied by the number of original heirs (n) to get k. So k must be the original value of the estate. But we cannot determine it just yet.

We can however equate these two expressions for the total estate, and then solve:

$$
\begin{aligned}
300{,}000n &= 250{,}000(n + 1) \\
300{,}000n &= 250{,}000n + 250{,}000 \\
50{,}000n &= 250{,}000 \\
n &= 5.
\end{aligned}
$$

So there were five original heirs. Thus the original estate was worth five times $\$300{,}000$, or 1.5 million dollars.

e. Reason quantitatively and use units to solve problems (i.e., dimensional analysis)

1. What does it mean to reason quantitatively?

Quantitative reasoning can mean a variety of things. As opposed to qualitative reasoning, it could mean using specific numbers to draw conclusions. For instance, one of the Sample Problems above asked what would happen to the volume of a sphere if its radius were doubled. An answer like, "the volume would increase," though technically correct, would be more of a qualitative response. A better answer is more quantitative in this case, "the volume would increase by a factor of 8."

Quantitative reasoning could also be viewed as one part of more general logical thinking. For example, statistical evidence can provide support to a variety of arguments, especially those involving decisions in public policy-making. Having an awareness and understanding of quantity and relative size can go a long way towards a deeper understanding of the world around us.

2. What is dimensional analysis? How does it work?

Dimensional analysis is a tool that I first really learned about as a physics student - physicists find this tool useful. It can help you find an answer if you do not know another method, or it can serve as a check to see if your answer might be correct. The saying "You can't add apples and oranges" is part of this line of reasoning. There are a few rules as to how you can do arithmetic on real-world quantities, and how the dimensions, or units, on the answer behave. We will list some of them below, with brief explanations. Note that a "pure number", like 3 or π, is a number that has no units to it.

- You cannot add or subtract two quantities unless they have the same units. Two quantities are not equal unless they have the same units.

  It doesn't make sense to add 2 centimeters to 3 seconds. One is a length measurement, the other is time. Here is where the "apples and oranges" comment fits in. Now, if you change your view so that the units are "pieces of fruit" then yes, you can add apples and oranges because they are both pieces of fruit. It also does not make sense to say that 2 cm equals 2 seconds. These quantities cannot be compared.

- When multiplying or dividing quantities, their units multiply or divide, respectively.

  For example, the area of a rectangle is the product of its length and its width. If length and width are in feet, then the area will have units of (feet)(feet), or square feet (ft^2). Similarly, if a city is growing at a rate of 2000 people per year for 4 years, then the total growth of the city over that period would be

$$\left(2000 \ \frac{\text{people}}{\text{year}}\right)(4 \text{ years}) = 8000 \ \frac{\text{people}}{\text{year}} \cdot \text{years} = 8000 \text{ people}.$$

- You can only raise a quantity to a pure number power, in which case its units are also raised to that power.

  It doesn't make sense to raise four kilograms to the centimeter power. Exponents must be dimensionless.

- (more advanced) The input and output values of a transcendental function (like logarithms and trigonometric functions) must be pure numbers.

  This is more advanced, and may seem to be a rule that is broken in physics, where quantities like $\cos t$, where t is time, might show up in wave theory. However, usually when terms like $\cos t$ appear, it is because of a very particular choice of units, or a mathematical simplification by ignoring a physical constant that might have a value of 1, even though it is not dimensionless. A more precise formula would involve $\cos \omega t$, where ω is the frequency, and has units of "1 over time", such as seconds^{-1}, also known as Hertz (Hz). This way, the units cancel and you can take the cosine of a pure number. (Incidentally, radian measure is also a pure number, being a ratio of two lengths. Degrees are a unit. This is another reason why mathematics teachers like to use radians rather than degrees.)

  Also, it may seem like the output of $\cos \omega t$ might be the intensity of a sound, or something else that has units. How can this be when cosine has to be a pure number? Again, a better, more precise formula would be $A \cos \omega t$, where A is the amplitude and possesses the relevant units.

  Again, this last bullet point may seem beyond the scope of basic dimensional analysis, but I include it here as a guide to where this topic leads in more advanced science and engineering coursework.

3. What are some examples of how to solve problems using dimensional analysis?

   Let's look at a few examples. First, let's calculate how many seconds there are in a week. These kinds of conversion problems are a good application of unit equivalences. Using the Factor-Label method (often taught in Chemistry), we multiply one week by successive fractions that are equal to 1 until we arrive at a quantity with the units of seconds.

$$(1 \text{ week}) \cdot \left(\frac{7 \text{ days}}{1 \text{ week}}\right) \cdot \left(\frac{24 \text{ hours}}{1 \text{ day}}\right) \cdot \left(\frac{60 \text{ minutes}}{1 \text{ hour}}\right) \cdot \left(\frac{60 \text{ seconds}}{1 \text{ minute}}\right) = 7 \cdot 24 \cdot 60 \cdot 60 \text{ seconds},$$

   which is 604,800 seconds. Notice how all the unit labels cancel out except for seconds.

As a different kind of example, suppose you drove a total of m miles and it took you h hours. Find your average speed for the trip. I'll give you four choices: $m + h, mh, \dfrac{m}{h}, \dfrac{h}{m}$. Which one is correct?

Well, using dimensional analysis, we can rule out $m + h$ as impossible. What would its units be? You can't add miles to hours. The second option, mh, is possible, but its units would be (miles)(hours), which are not units of speed. The third option, $\dfrac{m}{h}$, has units of $\dfrac{\text{miles}}{\text{hours}}$, or miles per hour, which are certainly units of speed. This might be the right answer. The fourth option, $\dfrac{h}{m}$, has units of hours per mile, which would describe how many hours it took to drive one mile. While this is certainly related to speed (inversely related, in fact), it does not have units of speed in the way we usually measure speed. So the third option, $\dfrac{m}{h}$, must be the correct one.

Notice that we didn't have to actually know the formula that rate times time equals distance. We only had to know that speed in this situation would be measured in miles per hour. Even in the absence of four choices, students might have come up with $\dfrac{m}{h}$ on their own. While this is the correct answer in this case, it is worth noting that just because the units are correct, does not necessarily mean that the formula is correct: $\dfrac{2m}{h}$ and $\dfrac{m}{2h}$ also have the correct units, but give the wrong answer. However, dimensional analysis can often be used to determine if you have an incorrect answer.

As a second example, let's consider the formula for the height of a projectile as a function of time: $h = -\frac{1}{2}gt^2 + v_0 t + h_0$. If the height is in feet and time is in seconds, find the dimensions of g, v_0, and h_0.

So, since h has units of feet, and since h is a sum of three terms, each of these terms must have units of feet. So $-\frac{1}{2}gt^2, v_0 t$, and h_0 all have units of feet. Since $v_0 t$ has units of feet and t has units of seconds, v_0 must be in feet per second in order to have the dimension of seconds cancel out when v_0 and t are multiplied together. (So this means v_0 must be a velocity of some sort.) Finally, $-\frac{1}{2}gt^2$ also has units of feet. So, g has units of feet divided by seconds squared, or feet per second per second. (Thus g describes a change in a velocity over time, also known as acceleration.)

Notice that if we were having trouble remembering where the acceleration and velocity pieces go in this formula, dimensional analysis can help us sort it out.

4. Sample Problems

   (a) The speed limit on a local highway is 65 miles per hour. How many feet per second is that?

   (b) A lighthouse rotates once every 53 seconds. How many times will it rotate in an eight-hour period?

   (c) Suppose a student comes to you with the following expression that will give the radius of the earth (in km): $2t/27$, where t is the length of one day, in seconds. The student says the numbers agree. The student claims to have discovered some new physics. What do you tell the student?

5. Answers to Sample Problems

(a) The speed limit on a local highway is 65 miles per hour. How many feet per second is that? 95.33 feet per second

$$\left(\frac{65 \text{ miles}}{1 \text{ hr}}\right) \cdot \left(\frac{1 \text{ hr}}{60 \text{ min}}\right) \cdot \left(\frac{1 \text{ min}}{60 \text{ sec}}\right) \cdot \left(\frac{5280 \text{ ft}}{1 \text{ mile}}\right) = \frac{65 \cdot 5280 \text{ ft}}{60 \cdot 60 \text{ sec}},$$

which is 95.33 feet per second.

(b) A lighthouse rotates once every 53 seconds. How many times will it rotate in an eight-hour period? 543.

$$\left(\frac{1 \text{ rot}}{53 \text{ sec}}\right) \cdot \left(\frac{60 \text{ sec}}{1 \text{ min}}\right) \cdot \left(\frac{60 \text{ min}}{1 \text{ hr}}\right)(8 \text{ hrs}) = \frac{60 \cdot 60 \cdot 8 \text{rot}}{53} \approx 543.39 \text{ rot.}$$

The lighthouse makes 543 complete rotations in an eight-hour period (plus a little more).

(c) Suppose a student comes to you with the following expression that will give the radius of the earth (in km): $2t/27$, where t is the length of one day, in seconds. The student says the numbers agree. The student claims to have discovered some new physics. What do you tell the student?

The student is just relating some numbers. Yes, the numbers are pretty close. There are 86,400 seconds in a day, and so $2(86,400)/27 = 6400$, which is approximately the radius of the earth in kilometers. But the units are not compatible. The formula given by the student has units of time, not length. So it doesn't make sense as is.

But the student can alter their formula to make the units correct. By saying $R = \dfrac{(2 \text{ km})t}{27 \text{ sec}}$, then at least the units work out, but now the true physics question is: what is the significance of 2 km and 27 seconds? Why should those numbers be important? Physics is more than just a collection of formulas that describe the universe on many different scales. A formula must be generalizable in its applicability in order to rise to the level of a powerful physical formula.

f. Perform operations on complex numbers and represent complex numbers and their operations on the complex plane

1. What is the definition of a real number? . . . of an imaginary number? . . . of a complex number?

A real number can be thought of as any point on the number line. (See section **a.** above.) Sometimes people point out that real numbers satisfy $x^2 \geq 0$.

An imaginary number is one satisfying $x^2 \leq 0$. If we let $\mathbf{i}^2 = -1$, then imaginary numbers can be written as $b\mathbf{i}$, where b is real. [There is sometimes a debate on whether 0 is imaginary or not. I choose to think of 0 as $0\mathbf{i}$ in this case, making it imaginary. It's also real. No one said that numbers had to be either real or imaginary, but not both.]

A complex number can be expressed as the sum of a real number and an imaginary number. So, any complex number can be written as $a + b\mathbf{i}$, where a and b are real numbers.

2. How can you add, subtract or multiply complex numbers?

   Complex numbers follow the usual rules of operations and algebra, only we have to remember that $\mathbf{i}^2 = -1$. Let's consider $w = 2 - 3\mathbf{i}$ and $z = 5 + 4\mathbf{i}$. Then

   $$
   \begin{aligned}
   w + z &= (2 - 3\mathbf{i}) + (5 + 4\mathbf{i}) = 2 + 5 + (-3\mathbf{i} + 4\mathbf{i}) = 7 + \mathbf{i} \\
   w - z &= (2 - 3\mathbf{i}) - (5 + 4\mathbf{i}) = 2 - 5 + (-3\mathbf{i} - 4\mathbf{i}) = -3 - 7\mathbf{i} \\
   wz &= (2 - 3\mathbf{i})(5 + 4\mathbf{i}) = 10 + 8\mathbf{i} - 15\mathbf{i} - 12\mathbf{i}^2 = 10 - 7\mathbf{i} - 12(-1) = 22 - 7\mathbf{i}.
   \end{aligned}
   $$

   Notice that multiples of $\mathbf{i}$ are like terms.

3. How do you divide complex numbers?

   Before we talk about division, let's recall that the *complex conjugate* of $a + b\mathbf{i}$ is $a - b\mathbf{i}$. This will come in handy in order to write a quotient of complex numbers in $a + b\mathbf{i}$ form. In particular, we will multiply a quotient by a fraction equal to 1 (namely, the conjugate of the denominator divided by itself) and then simplify our answer. Using the same w and z from above,

   $$
   \frac{w}{z} = \frac{2 - 3\mathbf{i}}{5 + 4\mathbf{i}}\left(\frac{5 - 4\mathbf{i}}{5 - 4\mathbf{i}}\right) = \frac{(2 - 3\mathbf{i})(5 - 4\mathbf{i})}{(5 + 4\mathbf{i})(5 - 4\mathbf{i})} = \frac{10 - 8\mathbf{i} - 15\mathbf{i} + 12\mathbf{i}^2}{25 + 20\mathbf{i} - 20\mathbf{i} - 16\mathbf{i}^2} = \frac{-2 - 23\mathbf{i}}{41},
   $$

   which can be written in $a + b\mathbf{i}$ form as $\dfrac{w}{z} = -\dfrac{2}{41} - \dfrac{23}{41}\mathbf{i}$.

4. How do you find roots of complex numbers?

   Finding complex roots requires trigonometry and an understanding of DeMoivre's Theorem. See details in the Trigonometry section in the study guide for CSET III, subsection **5.1.e**.

5. What is the complex plane?

   The complex plane is a way of visualizing complex numbers on a two-dimensional Cartesian plane. The x-axis is called the "real" axis and the y-axis is called the "imaginary" axis. Complex numbers then correspond to points on the complex plane. The number $-2\mathbf{i}$ corresponds to the point $(0, -2)$, while $3 + 3\mathbf{i}$ corresponds to $(3, 3)$. Real numbers (with imaginary part equal to 0) lie on the real axis. See the picture below.

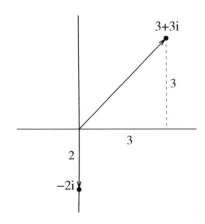

6. How do you represent addition or subtraction on the complex plane?

Addition on the complex plane can be thought of in the language of vectors. Please see section **2.4.a** (below) for more information about how vectors add and subtract.

Essentially, one adds vectors componentwise. In complex numbers, this means that one adds the real parts and imaginary parts separately. Geometrically, one adds vectors by placing the tail of one vector at the head of another. Subtraction is similar, except that we think of subtraction as adding the additive inverse. So, we add a vector that points in the opposite direction to the vector being subtracted.

In the picture, we have demonstrated $v + w$ and $v - w$, where $v = 1 - 2i$ and $w = 3 + 3i$. Algebraically, we get $v + w = 4 + i$ and $v - w = -2 - 5i$.

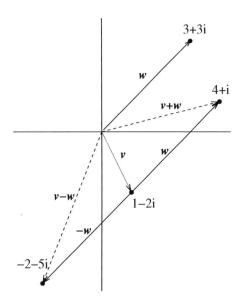

7. How do you represent multiplication on the complex plane?

Please see the Trigonometry subsection **5.1.e** for information on the polar form of complex numbers. For now, we will just say that because of trigonometry, we can write complex numbers either in $a + bi$ form, or in so-called polar form, as $re^{i\theta}$. In polar form, r is the distance to the origin, and θ is the angle between the positive real axis and the line segment having one endpoint at the origin and the other at the complex number in question.

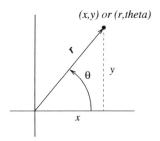

The first form is better for addition and subtraction of complex numbers graphically, because the real and imaginary parts correspond to horizontal and vertical displacements, respectively.

The second form is better for multiplication of complex numbers graphically, because it relies on geometric properties of the line segments corresponding to the complex numbers. Consider the equation:

$$(r_1 e^{i\theta_1})(r_2 e^{i\theta_2}) = (r_1 r_2)e^{i(\theta_1+\theta_2)},$$

From here, we see that the line segment corresponding to the product has the following properties:

- Its length is the product of the lengths corresponding to the factors.

- Its angle is the sum of the angles corresponding to the factors.

So, to multiply two complex numbers graphically, one multiplies their line segment lengths and adds their angles. The result is a line segment that identifies the product. Using the same v and w as before, we show vw. Algebraically, we get $vw = (1-2i)(3+3i) = 3-6i+3i-6i^2 = 9-3i$. Using polar form we get

$$vw = (\sqrt{5}e^{i\alpha})(3\sqrt{2}e^{i\theta}) = 3\sqrt{10}e^{i(\alpha+\theta)}.$$

Note that $\theta = \frac{\pi}{4}$, but that $\alpha \approx 5.176$ radians.

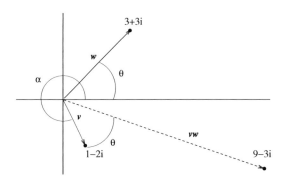

8. How do you represent division on the complex plane?

If we use the polar representation of a complex number, then it is relatively easy to perform division.

$$\frac{r_1 e^{i\theta_1}}{r_2 e^{i\theta_2}} = \left(\frac{r_1}{r_2}\right) e^{i(\theta_1-\theta_2)}.$$

So, the line segment corresponding to the quotient has the following properties:

- Its length is a quotient: the length corresponding to the dividend divided by the length corresponding to the divisor.

- Its angle is a difference: the angle corresponding to the dividend minus the angle corresponding to the divisor.

Notice that these properties are the inverse of the properties under multiplication. So, to divide two complex numbers graphically, one divides their line segment lengths and subtracts their angles. The result is a line segment that identifies the product. Using the same v and w as before, we show $\frac{v}{w}$. Geometrically,

$$\frac{v}{w} = \frac{\sqrt{5}e^{i\alpha}}{3\sqrt{2}e^{i\theta}} = \frac{\sqrt{10}}{6}e^{i(\alpha-\theta)},$$

while algebraically,

$$\frac{v}{w} = \frac{1-2\mathbf{i}}{3+3\mathbf{i}} = \left(\frac{1-2\mathbf{i}}{3+3\mathbf{i}}\right)\cdot\left(\frac{3-3\mathbf{i}}{3-3\mathbf{i}}\right) = \frac{-3-9\mathbf{i}}{18} = -\frac{1}{6} - \frac{1}{2}\mathbf{i}.$$

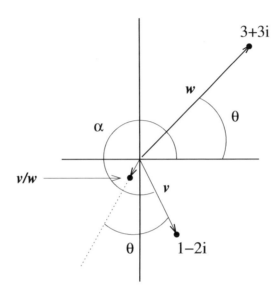

9. Sample Problems

  (a) Is the length of the line segment corresponding to $\frac{1}{z}$ the reciprocal of the length of the line segment corresponding to z? If so, why? Is the angle of the line segment corresponding to $\frac{1}{z}$ the negative of the angle of the line segment corresponding to z? If so, why?

  (b) For this problem, let $w = 3 - \mathbf{i}$, $v = -1 - 5\mathbf{i}$, and $z = 5 + 5\mathbf{i}$. Calculate the following:

    i. $w + v$
    ii. wv
    iii. $3w - 2\mathbf{i}z$
    iv. z^2
    v. $w\overline{w}$ (where $\overline{w}$ denotes the complex conjugate of w)
    vi. $\dfrac{v}{w}$
    vii. r and θ if $z = re^{i\theta}$

  (c) Let z be a complex number. Show that $z + \overline{z}$ and $z\overline{z}$ are always real.

10. Answers to Sample Problems

(a) Is the length of the line segment corresponding to $\dfrac{1}{z}$ the reciprocal of the length of the line segment corresponding to z? If so, why? Is the angle of the line segment corresponding to $\dfrac{1}{z}$ the negative of the angle of the line segment corresponding to z? If so, why? Yes and yes. As to why these conditions are correct, we can derive them directly.

If $z = re^{i\theta}$, then $\dfrac{1}{z} = \dfrac{1}{re^{i\theta}} = \dfrac{1}{r}e^{-i\theta}$. So the length is $\dfrac{1}{r}$ and the angle is $-\theta$.

(b) For this problem, let $w = 3 - i$, $v = -1 - 5i$, and $z = 5 + 5i$. Calculate the following:

   i. $w + v = 2 - 6i$

   ii. $wv = -8 - 14i$

   iii. $3w - 2iz = 19 - 13i$

   iv. $z^2 = 50i$

   v. $w\overline{w} = 10$ (where $\overline{w}$ denotes the complex conjugate of w)

   vi. $\dfrac{v}{w} = \dfrac{2 - 16i}{10} = \dfrac{1}{5} - \dfrac{8}{5}i$

   vii. r and θ if $z = re^{i\theta}$; $r = 5\sqrt{2}, \theta = \dfrac{\pi}{4}$

(c) Let z be a complex number. Show that $z + \overline{z}$ and $z\overline{z}$ are always real. Let $z = a + bi$. Then $\overline{z} = a - bi$. So

$$z + \overline{z} = (a + bi) + (a - bi) = 2a; \quad z\overline{z} = (a + bi)(a - bi) = a^2 - b^2 i^2 = a^2 + b^2$$

There are no terms involving i in the final answers. So $z + \overline{z}$ and $z\overline{z}$ are real.

1.2 Number Theory

a. Prove and use basic properties of natural numbers (e.g., properties of divisibility)

1. What are the natural numbers?

$$\mathbb{N} = \{1, 2, 3, 4, 5, \ldots\}$$

(Often, computer science books include zero in the natural numbers, but most mathematics books do not.) In higher mathematics, the natural numbers are built out of other objects, like sets. Then, the natural numbers are used to define the integers, which are then used to define the rational numbers, which are then used to define the real numbers, which are then used to define the complex numbers. See **1.1.a** and **1.1.f** for more details.

2. What are some axioms of the natural numbers?

(Remember, axioms do not need to be proved.)

The natural numbers are closed under addition and multiplication, which are commutative and associate operations in which multiplication distributes over addition. Also, the natural numbers are well ordered, which means that if a and b are natural numbers, then either $a \leq b$ or $b \leq a$. It also means that there is a smallest element.

3. What is division in the natural numbers (or integers)?

There is a Division Algorithm in the integers that says the following. If a and b are natural numbers, then there exist *unique* integers q and r (called the *quotient* and *remainder*) satisfying

   (a) $a = qb + r$, and

   (b) $0 \leq r < b$.

Usually, $a \geq b$, although that is not technically necessary. Also, a could be any integer and division would still work.

4. What is divisibility in the natural numbers (or integers)?

Let a and b be natural numbers [respectively, integers], with $b \neq 0$. We say a is **divisible** by b, or b **divides** a, or $b|a$, if there exists a natural number [resp., integer] k satisfying $a = bk$. In other words, the remainder is zero when a is divided by b.

5. What are some properties of divisibility?

Let $a, b, c \in \mathbb{N}$.

   (a) $a|a$.

   (b) If $a|b$ and $b|c$, then $a|c$.

   (c) If $a|b$, then $a|bc$.

   (d) If $c|a$ and $c|b$, then $c|a + b$.

6. Sample Problems

    (a) Let $a, b \in \mathbb{N}$. Prove that the geometric mean of a and b is less than or equal to the arithmetic mean of a and b; that is, $\sqrt{ab} \leq \frac{a+b}{2}$.

    (b) Let $a, b \in \mathbb{N}$. Prove that $\sqrt{ab} = \frac{a+b}{2}$ if and only if $a = b$.

    (c) Prove that a number is divisible by 4 if the number formed by its last two digits is divisible by 4.

    (d) Prove that a number is divisible by 3 if the sum of its digits is divisible by 3. (You may assume the number has three digits, although the property is true in general.)

    (e) Prove that there are an infinite number of Pythagorean triples.

7. Answers to Sample Problems

    (a) Let $a, b \in \mathbb{N}$. Prove that the geometric mean of a and b is less than or equal to the arithmetic mean of a and b; that is, $\sqrt{ab} \leq \frac{a+b}{2}$.

    Since $a - b$ is a real number, $(a-b)^2 \geq 0$. So,

$$
\begin{aligned}
a^2 - 2ab + b^2 &\geq 0 \\
a^2 + 2ab + b^2 &\geq 4ab \\
(a+b)^2 &\geq 4ab \\
a + b &\geq 2\sqrt{ab},
\end{aligned}
$$

where the last step follows because $ab > 0$. Dividing both sides by 2 gives the final result.

    (b) Let $a, b \in \mathbb{N}$. Prove that $\sqrt{ab} = \frac{a+b}{2}$ if and only if $a = b$.

    Multiplying both sides by 2 and then squaring both sides, we get $4ab = a^2 + 2ab + b^2$, or $0 = a^2 - 2ab + b^2 = (a-b)^2$. Thus $a - b$ must equal zero, that is, $a = b$.

    (c) Prove that a number is divisible by 4 if the number formed by its last two digits is divisible by 4.

    Since 100 is divisible by 4, we know that any number times 100 is also divisible by 4. (See properties of divisibility, above.) So we can disregard the digits in the hundreds place and higher, since they will not affect whether the overall number is divisible by 4. Only the tens and ones digits matter. As an example, consider $3424 = 34(100) + 24$. We know that 4 divides 100, and thus $34(100)$ as well. So, 3424 is divisible by 4 if and only if 24 is divisible by 4, which it is. So 3424 is divisible by 4.

    (d) Prove that a number is divisible by 3 if the sum of its digits is divisible by 3. (You may assume the number has three digits, although the property is true in general.)

    Let h, t, and u be the hundreds, tens, and ones digits of the number n. Then

$$
n = 100h + 10t + u = (h + t + u) + 99h + 9t.
$$

    Suppose that the digit sum of n is divisible by 3. Then $h + t + u = 3k$ for some integer k. Then $n = 3k + 99h + 9t = 3(k + 33h + 3t)$. Clearly, n is divisible by 3. As an aside, notice that a similar argument shows that n is divisible by 9 if its digit sum is divisible by 9.

(e) Prove that there are an infinite number of Pythagorean triples.

The easy way to prove this is to prove that $(3, 4, 5)$ is a Pythagorean triple first $[3^2 + 4^2 = 9 + 16 = 25 = 5^2]$. Then we can show that $(3k, 4k, 5k)$ is another Pythagorean triple for any value of k. Indeed,

$$(3k)^2 + (4k)^2 = 9k^2 + 16k^2 = 25k^2 = (5k)^2.$$

So, $(6, 8, 10)$, $(9, 12, 15)$, etc. belong to an infinite chain of Pythagorean triples.

The harder way is to show that there are an infinite number of Pythagorean triples *no two of which are multiples of each other*. Let's look at the difference between consecutive squares.

$$(n + 1)^2 - n^2 = n^2 + 2n + 1 - n^2 = 2n + 1$$

This means that every positive odd number, because it can be written as $2n + 1$, is the difference between two consecutive squares. For example, $4^2 - 3^2 = 16 - 9 = 7$. So $7 = 2(3) + 1$ is a difference of two consecutive squares. But 7 is not itself a perfect square, which means we do not get a Pythagorean triple in this case. However, $9 = 2(4) + 1$ is an odd number and a perfect square. In fact, $5^2 - 4^2 = 25 - 16 = 9 = 3^2$, which gives us the Pythagorean triple $(3, 4, 5)$. The next odd square is $25 = 2(12) + 1$. So $13^2 - 12^2 = 169 - 144 = 25 = 5^2$, giving $(5, 12, 13)$ as a Pythagorean triple. The next one in this sequence is $(7, 24, 25)$. Since there are an infinite number of odd perfect squares, we will get an infinite number of Pythagorean triples, no two of which are multiples of each other.

b. Use the Principle of Mathematical Induction to prove results in number theory

1. What is Mathematical Induction?

   If you have a sequence of statements $(S_1, S_2, S_3, \dots)$ that satisfy the following properties: (1) that S_1 is true, and (2) that if S_k is true, then it follows that S_{k+1} is also true for all $k \in \mathbb{N}$, then the Principle of Mathematical Induction says that every statement in the sequence is true.

2. What is Complete Induction?

   If you have a sequence of statements $(S_1, S_2, S_3, \dots)$ that satisfy the following properties: (1) that S_1 is true, and (2) that if S_j is true for all $j \leq k$, then it follows that S_{k+1} is also true for all $k \in \mathbb{N}$, then the Principle of Complete Induction says that every statement in the sequence is true.

   The difference here is that in Complete Induction, you are allowed to assume that all the previous statements are true, rather than just the immediate predecessor. This can be very useful if one statement depends on several preceding statements.

3. How does one prove a result by induction?

   To prove a result by induction, one must prove the two parts of the principle. First, one must prove that S_1 is true. Second, one must prove that *if* S_k is true, for some value of k, then S_{k+1} must also be true.

4. Sample Problems (Prove the following statements.)

(a) $\sum_{i=1}^{n} i = \dfrac{n(n+1)}{2}$ for all $n \in \mathbb{N}$.

(b) The number $n^3 - n$ is divisible by 6 for any natural number n.

(c) $13 | (14^n - 1)$ for all $n \in \mathbb{N}$.

(d) $\sum_{i=1}^{n} i^2 = \dfrac{n(n+1)(2n+1)}{6}$ for all $n \in \mathbb{N}$.

(e) The sum of the even integers from 2 to $2n$ is $n(n+1)$.

(f) $\sum_{i=0}^{n} 2^i = 2^{n+1} - 1$ for all $n \in \mathbb{N}$.

5. Answers to Sample Problems

(a) $\sum_{i=1}^{n} i = \dfrac{n(n+1)}{2}$ for all $n \in \mathbb{N}$.

Proof: First, we must show that $\sum_{i=1}^{1} i = \dfrac{1(1+1)}{2}$. But $\sum_{i=1}^{1} i = 1 = \dfrac{1(2)}{2}$. So the statement S_1 is true.

Aside: What is the general statement, S_n?

ANS: S_n is the statement we are asked to prove at the beginning, namely

$$\sum_{i=1}^{n} i = \frac{n(n+1)}{2} \text{ for all } n \in \mathbb{N}.$$

Second, we need to show that if S_k is true for some k, then S_{k+1} is also true. So, we assume that S_k is true for some k. That is, $\sum_{i=1}^{k} i = \dfrac{k(k+1)}{2}$. This will come in handy later. Now we must prove that S_{k+1} is true under this assumption. We will start by looking at the sum of i as i ranges from 1 to $k+1$ and we will algebraically manipulate it to fit the desired formula.

$$
\begin{aligned}
\sum_{i=1}^{k+1} i &= \left(\sum_{i=1}^{k} i \right) + (k+1) \\
&= \frac{k(k+1)}{2} + (k+1) \\
&= (k+1)\left(\frac{k}{2} + 1 \right) \\
&= \frac{(k+1)(k+2)}{2},
\end{aligned}
$$

which exactly proves that S_{k+1} is true. Therefore, the Principle of Mathematical Induction implies that S_n is true for all n, namely, that $\sum_{i=1}^{n} i = \dfrac{n(n+1)}{2}$. $\square$

(b) The number $n^3 - n$ is divisible by 6 for any natural number n.

Proof: S_1 says that $1^3 - 1$ is divisible by 6. That is true, because $1^3 - 1 = 0 = 6(0)$. Now assume that $k^3 - k$ is divisible by 6, which means that $k^3 - k = 6m$ for some integer m. Consider

$$(k+1)^3 - (k+1) = k^3 + 3k^2 + 3k + 1 - k - 1 = (k^3 - k) + 3k(k+1) = 6m + 3k(k+1),$$

where we used the assumption that $k^3 - k$ is divisible by 6. Notice that for any k, either k or $k+1$ must be even, which means that $3k(k+1)$ is also divisible by 6. Thus, $(k+1)^3 - (k+1)$ is divisible by 6. Therefore, by the Principle of Mathematical Induction, $n^3 - n$ is divisible by 6 for all n. $\square$

(c) $13 \mid (14^n - 1)$ for all $n \in \mathbb{N}$.

Proof: Clearly, $14^1 - 1 = 13$ is divisible by 13. Let's now assume that $14^k - 1$ is divisible by 13. So, $14^k - 1 = 13m$ for some integer m. Then

$$14^{k+1} - 1 = 14(14^k) - 1 = (13+1)(14^k) - 1 = 13(14^k) + (14^k - 1) = 13(14^k) + 13m.$$

Since each term is divisible by 13, then $14^{k+1} - 1$ is also divisible by 13. Therefore, the Principle of Mathematical Induction says that $13 \mid (14^n - 1)$ for all $n \in \mathbb{N}$. $\square$

(d) $\displaystyle\sum_{i=1}^{n} i^2 = \dfrac{n(n+1)(2n+1)}{6}$ for all $n \in \mathbb{N}$.

Proof: When $n = 1$, both sides are equal to 1. So assume that $\displaystyle\sum_{i=1}^{k} i^2 = \dfrac{k(k+1)(2k+1)}{6}$ for some $k \in \mathbb{N}$. Then

$$
\begin{aligned}
\sum_{i=1}^{k+1} i^2 &= \left(\sum_{i=1}^{k} i^2 \right) + (k+1)^2 \\
&= \frac{k(k+1)(2k+1)}{6} + (k+1)^2 \\
&= \left(\frac{k+1}{6} \right) [k(2k+1) + 6(k+1)] \\
&= \left(\frac{k+1}{6} \right) (2k^2 + 7k + 6) \\
&= \frac{(k+1)(k+2)(2k+3)}{6} = \frac{(k+1)((k+1)+1)(2(k+1)+1)}{6},
\end{aligned}
$$

which is exactly the formula we wanted. Therefore, the Principle of Mathematical Induction says that $\displaystyle\sum_{i=1}^{n} i^2 = \dfrac{n(n+1)(2n+1)}{6}$ for all $n \in \mathbb{N}$. $\square$

(e) The sum of the even integers from 2 to $2n$ is $n(n+1)$.

This is the same proof as problem (a), above, except with both sides multiplied by 2.

(f) $\displaystyle\sum_{i=0}^{n} 2^i = 2^{n+1} - 1$ for all $n \in \mathbb{N}$.

Proof: Let $n = 1$. Then $\displaystyle\sum_{i=0}^{1} 2^i = 2^0 + 2^1 = 3 = 2^2 - 1$. So the statement is true when $n = 1$. Assume the statement is true for some $k \in \mathbb{N}$. That means that $\displaystyle\sum_{i=0}^{k} 2^i = 2^{k+1} - 1$. Then

$$
\begin{aligned}
\sum_{i=0}^{k+1} 2^i &= \left(\sum_{i=0}^{k} 2^i\right) + 2^{k+1} \\
&= (2^{k+1} - 1) + 2^{k+1} \\
&= 2(2^{k+1}) - 1 = 2^{k+2} - 1,
\end{aligned}
$$

which is exactly the formula we wanted. Therefore the Principle of Mathematical Induction says that $\displaystyle\sum_{i=0}^{n} 2^i = 2^{n+1} - 1$ for all $n \in \mathbb{N}$.

c. Apply the Euclidean Algorithm

1. What is the Euclidean Algorithm?

   The Euclidean Algorithm is a procedure that returns the greatest common factor (or greatest common divisor, GCD) of two given natural numbers. The input is two natural numbers a and b, with $a \geq b$. The output is the largest natural number which is a factor of both numbers.

2. How does the Euclidean Algorithm work?

   The Euclidean Algorithm (GCD) is a recursive algorithm that can be summarized as follows:

   To find the greatest common factor of a and b (where $a \geq b$), first divide a by b to find q and r satisfying $a = qb + r$ and $0 \leq r < b$. If $r = 0$, then $GCD(a, b) = b$. If $r \neq 0$, then $GCD(a, b) = GCD(b, r)$.

   Example: Find $GCD(15, 6)$.

   ANS: Since $15 = 2(6) + 3$, then $r \neq 0$. So $GCD(15, 6) = GCD(6, 3)$. We repeat the algorithm. Since $6 = 2(3) + 0$, $GCD(6, 3) = 3$. Thus $GCD(15, 6) = 3$.

3. Why does the Euclidean Algorithm work?

   Since $b > r$ at each step, meaning the next remainder $r' < r$, and so on, we have a descending chain of natural numbers: $b, r, r', \ldots$. But in the natural numbers, such a chain has to be finite. There are only a finite number of natural number solutions to $x < b$ for any value of b. Therefore the algorithm will eventually stop.

The algorithm stops at the right answer because the common factors of a and b are exactly the same as the common factors of b and r. This is because $a = qb + r$, and thus $r = a - qb$. If d is a factor of a and b, then d is a factor of $a - qb = r$ as well. Conversely, if d is a factor of b and r, then d is a factor of $qb + r = a$. Since no common factors are gained or lost, the greatest common factor of the original two numbers is preserved through every step of the algorithm.

4. What is an application of Euclidean Algorithm?

   USEFUL FACT: The greatest common factor of a and b is the smallest natural number that can be written as $as + bt$, where s and t are suitably chosen integers. (The integers s and t are not unique, but you can find suitable values via the Euclidean Algorithm.)

5. Sample Problems

   (a) Find the greatest common factor of 123 and 24.

   (b) Find the greatest common factor of 55 and 34.

   (c) Find the greatest common factor of 91 and 35.

   (d) Show that the greatest common factor of $7n + 4$ and $5n + 3$ is 1 for all $n \in \mathbb{N}$.

6. Answers to Sample Problems

   (a) Find the greatest common factor of 123 and 24. 3
       Since $123 = 5(24) + 3$, $GCD(123, 24) = GCD(24, 3)$. Since $24 = 8(3)$, $GCD(24, 3) = 3$.

   (b) Find the greatest common factor of 55 and 34. 1
       $55 = 1(34) + 21; 34 = 1(21) + 13; 21 = 1(13) + 8; 13 = 1(8) + 5; 8 = 1(5) + 3;$
       $5 = 1(3) + 2; 3 = 1(2) + 1; 2 = 2(1) + 0.$

   (c) Find the greatest common factor of 91 and 35. 7
       $91 = 2(35) + 21; 35 = 1(21) + 14; 21 = 1(14) + 7; 14 = 2(7) + 0.$

   (d) Show that the greatest common factor of $7n + 4$ and $5n + 3$ is 1 for all $n \in \mathbb{N}$.
       $7n + 4 = 1(5n + 3) + (2n + 1); 5n + 3 = 2(2n + 1) + n + 1;$
       $2n + 1 = 2(n + 1) - 1; n + 1 = -(n + 1)(-1) + 0.$
       Or, $-5(7n + 4) + 7(5n + 3) = 1$, which means 1 is the greatest common factor. (See USEFUL FACT, above.)

d. Apply the Fundamental Theorem of Arithmetic (e.g., find the greatest common factor and the least common multiple; show that every fraction is equivalent to a unique fraction where the numerator and denominator are relatively prime; prove that the square root of any number, not a perfect square number, is irrational)

1. What is the Fundamental Theorem of Arithmetic?

   The Fundamental Theorem of Arithmetic states that if n is a natural number, then n can be expressed as a product of prime numbers. Moreover, there is only one way to do so, up to a permutation of the prime factors of n. (Here, we allow a "product" to consist of only one prime, or of no primes so that we can say that EVERY natural number, including 1, is a "product" of primes.)

2. What is a prime number?

   The number $n \in \mathbb{N}$ is **prime** if $n > 1$ and the only positive divisors of n are 1 and n. As examples, 7 is prime but 9 is not, because 9 has 3 as a divisor.

3. Why is the Fundamental Theorem of Arithmetic true?

   The first sentence can be proved using Complete Induction. The second sentence can be proved by using the following Helpful Fact.

   Helpful Fact: Let p be a prime. If $p|ab$, then $p|a$ or $p|b$.

   Proof: (of Helpful Fact) Suppose $p|ab$ but p does not divide a. Then the greatest common factor of p and a must be 1, because there are no other factors of p. By the USEFUL FACT, above, there must be integers s and t satisfying $1 = as + pt$. Multiplying both sides by b, we get $b = bas + bpt$. Notice that $p|bas$ (because $p|ab$) and clearly $p|bpt$. Therefore, $p|b$. □

4. How does one find the greatest common factor and the least common multiple, using the Fundamental Theorem of Arithmetic?

   Here, one can find the unique prime factorization of two numbers and use that information to determine the greatest common factor and the least common multiple. As an example, consider 12 and 18. We know $12 = 2^2 \cdot 3$ and $18 = 2 \cdot 3^2$. Both share a single factor of 2 and a single factor of 3. So, $2 \cdot 3 = 6$ is the greatest common factor. For the least common multiple, notice that we need factors of at least 2^2 and 3^2 in order to have both 12 and 18 as a factor. So, the least common multiple is $2^2 3^2 = 36$.

5. How can fractions be uniquely represented as a ratio of relatively prime integers? (What does relatively prime mean?)

   The numbers a and b are *relatively prime* if they have no common factors. This happens when $GCD(a, b) = 1$. If you are given a fraction, you can use the Fundamental Theorem of Arithmetic to write the numerator and denominator uniquely as products of primes. Then you can cancel any common factors between them. The resulting numerator and denominator will have no common factors, which makes them relatively prime.

6. What are some proofs that $\sqrt{2}$ is irrational?

   *** For a quick review of Proof by Contradiction, see the Miscellaneous Topics at the end of this book.

   (a) Euclid's proof

   (by contradiction) Assume that $\sqrt{2} = \frac{a}{b}$ and that a and b are relatively prime integers. Then $2b^2 = a^2$. Thus a^2 is even, which means that a has to be even. (The square of an odd number is odd.) So, $a = 2c$ for some integer c. Then $2b^2 = 4c^2$, which means $b^2 = 2c^2$. Thus b^2 is even, which means that b has to be even. But this is impossible, because a and b were chosen to be relatively prime; they can't both be even. Therefore, it must be impossible to write $\sqrt{2}$ as $\frac{a}{b}$, which means $\sqrt{2}$ is irrational.

   (b) Another proof

(by contradiction) Assume that $\sqrt{2} = \frac{a}{b}$. Then $2b^2 = a^2$. By the Fundamental Theorem of Arithmetic, the number on the left hand side of this equation must have an odd number of prime factors, and the number on the right hand side must have an even number of prime factors. This is impossible, because there is only one way to write a number (like $2b^2$) as a product of primes. Therefore, it must be impossible to write $\sqrt{2}$ as $\frac{a}{b}$, which means $\sqrt{2}$ is irrational.

7. Sample Problems

   (a) Consider $y = mx + b$, where m and b are rational numbers. Must there be a point on this line that has integer coordinates?

   (b) Consider $y = ax^2 + bx + c$, where a, b, and c are rational numbers. Must there be a point on this parabola that has integer coordinates?

   (c) Prove that $\sqrt{5}$ is irrational.

   (d) Prove or disprove: If x^2 is rational, then x is rational.

   (e) Prove or disprove: If x^2 is irrational, then x is irrational.

   (f) If $n = 2^2 3^3 x^5 y z^2$ and $m = 2^3 3^2 x^3 y^2$, then find the greatest common factor of n and m, and the least common multiple of n and m.

   (g) Show that if (x, y, z) is a Pythagorean triple, and if f is a common factor of x, y, and z, then $\left(\frac{x}{f}, \frac{y}{f}, \frac{z}{f}\right)$ is also a Pythagorean triple.

   (h) How many natural number solutions are there to $x + y = 12$? ... to $x + y = n \in \mathbb{N}$?

   (i) How many natural number solutions are there to $xy = 12$? ... to $xy = n \in \mathbb{N}$?

8. Answers to Sample Problems

   (a) Consider $y = mx + b$, where m and b are rational numbers. Must there be a point on this line that has integer coordinates?

   Not necessarily. For example, if $y = \frac{1}{3}x + \frac{1}{2}$, no matter what integer you plug in for x, y will not come out to an exact integer.

   (b) Consider $y = ax^2 + bx + c$, where a, b, and c are rational numbers. Must there be a point on this parabola that has integer coordinates?

   Not necessarily. The example given in the previous problem (with $a = 0$) still works. Also, if $a = b = c = \frac{1}{2}$, then for any integer x, y is equal to an integer plus $\frac{1}{2}$.

   (c) Prove that $\sqrt{5}$ is irrational. We can mimic the proof given above that $\sqrt{2}$ is irrational.
   Proof: Assume that $\sqrt{5} = \frac{a}{b}$. Then $5b^2 = a^2$. By the Fundamental Theorem of Arithmetic, the number on the left hand side of this equation must have an odd number of prime factors, and the number on the right hand side must have an even number of prime factors. This is impossible, because there is only one way to write a number (like $5b^2$) as a product of primes. Therefore, it must be impossible to write $\sqrt{5}$ as $\frac{a}{b}$, which means $\sqrt{5}$ is irrational.

(d) Prove or disprove: If x^2 is rational, then x is rational.

FALSE. Suppose $x^2 = 2$, which is rational. Then $x = \pm\sqrt{2}$, which was proven to be irrational. Thus the statement is false.

(e) Prove or disprove: If x^2 is irrational, then x is irrational.

Proof: Assume that x is rational. Then $x = \frac{p}{q}$ for some integers p and q, with $q \neq 0$. Then $x^2 = \frac{p^2}{q^2}$, which is clearly rational. Therefore, by indirect reasoning (contrapositive), we have shown that if x^2 is irrational, then x must be irrational too.

(f) If $n = 2^2 3^3 x^5 y z^2$ and $m = 2^3 3^2 x^3 y^2$, then find the greatest common factor of n and m, and the least common multiple of n and m.

The greatest common factor of n and m is $2^2 3^2 x^3 y$ and their least common multiple is $2^3 3^3 x^5 y^2 z^2$.

(g) Show that if (x, y, z) is a Pythagorean triple, and if f is a common factor of x, y, and z, then $\left(\frac{x}{f}, \frac{y}{f}, \frac{z}{f}\right)$ is also a Pythagorean triple.

$$\left(\frac{x}{f}\right)^2 + \left(\frac{y}{f}\right)^2 = \frac{x^2 + y^2}{f^2} = \frac{z^2}{f^2} = \left(\frac{z}{f}\right)^2$$

(h) How many natural number solutions are there to $x + y = 12$? ...to $x + y = n \in \mathbb{N}$? For the first equation, x can be any number between 1 and 11. So there are 11 solutions. (Some of these are essentially the same, like $1 + 11$ and $11 + 1$, but we ignore that similarity here because the solutions have distinct x-values.) For the second equation, then, there are $n - 1$ solutions.

(i) How many natural number solutions are there to $xy = 12$? ...to $xy = n \in \mathbb{N}$? For the first equation, there are 6 solutions, one for each factor of 12: $1, 2, 3, 4, 6, 12$. (Again, solutions are different if they have distinct x-values.) For the second equation, the answer is the number of factors of n. If n is prime, for example, then the answer is 2.

2.1 Algebraic Structures

a. Demonstrate knowledge of why the real and complex numbers are each a field, and that particular rings are not fields (e.g., integers, polynomial rings, matrix rings)

1. What is a field? What are some examples?

   A field is a set F together with two operations (called $+$ and $\times$) satisfying the following properties. Suppose that a, b, and c are elements of F.

   (a) F is closed under $+$ and $\times$

   This means that $a + b$ and $a \times b$, also called ab, are elements of F. [The element $a \times b$ is often written ab. We will follow this conventional notation below.]

   (b) $+$ and $\times$ are associative

   This means that $(a + b) + c = a + (b + c)$ and $(ab)c = a(bc)$.

   (c) $+$ and $\times$ are commutative

   This means that $a + b = b + a$ and $ab = ba$.

   (d) $+$ and $\times$ have identity elements 0 and 1 in F, respectively

   This means that $a + 0 = a$ and $b \cdot 1 = b$.

   (e) every element has an additive inverse in F

   This means that for every a in F, there is an element $-a$ **in** F satisfying $a + (-a) = 0$.

   (f) every non-zero element has a multiplicative inverse in F

   If $b \neq 0$, then there is $\frac{1}{b}$ **in** F satisfying $b(\frac{1}{b}) = 1$.

   (g) $\times$ distributes over $+$

   This means that $a(b + c) = ab + ac$.

   The most common fields we use are the rational numbers, the real numbers, and the complex numbers.

2. What is a ring? What are some examples?

   A ring is a set R together with two operations (called $+$ and $\times$) satisfying the following properties.

   (a) R is closed under $+$ and $\times$

   (b) $+$ and $\times$ are associative

   (c) $+$ is commutative

   (d) $+$ and $\times$ have identity elements 0 and 1 in R, respectively

   (e) every element has an additive inverse in R

   (f) $\times$ distributes over $+$

There are two key differences between the definition of a ring and the definition of a field: (1) rings do not necessarily have a commutative multiplication, and (2) rings do not necessarily contain multiplicative inverses. Notice that every field is a ring, but that there are rings which are not fields.

The most common rings we use (in addition to the fields listed above) are the integers, the set of square matrices of a given size (like all 2 by 2 matrices, for instance), and the set of polynomials with coefficients in another ring.

3. What are some non-examples of fields and rings?

The following common rings are not fields: integers, the set of square matrices of a given size (like all 2 by 2 matrices, for instance), and the set of polynomials with coefficients in another ring.

The natural numbers are not a ring. The set of all quadratic polynomials is not a ring. See Sample Problems, below.

4. Sample Problems

   (a) Give an example of a ring that is not a field.

   (b) Why are the integers not a field?

   (c) Why are the natural numbers not a ring?

   (d) Why is the set of all quadratic polynomials not a ring?

   (e) Write the multiplicative inverse of $3 - 2i$ in $a + bi$ form.

   (f) Show that the set of 2 by 2 matrices with integer entries forms a non-commutative ring.

   (g) Prove that the set of 2 by 2 invertible matrices with complex number entries is NOT a field.

   (h) Write the multiplicative inverse of $x + yi$ in $a + bi$ form.

   (i) What is the smallest field that contains 0 and 1?

   (j) Using the field properties listed above, prove that $(a + b)c = ac + bc$.

   (k) Let F be the field of rational functions $\dfrac{p(x)}{q(x)}$, where $p(x)$ and $q(x)$ are any polynomials with real coefficients and $q(x) \neq 0$.

        i. Show that F contains a multiplicative identity element.

        ii. Show that F is closed under multiplication.

        iii. Show that F is closed under addition.

        iv. Show that every non-zero element of F is invertible.

5. Answers to Sample Problems

   (a) Give an example of a ring that is not a field. Examples include: the integers, polynomials, and the set of all square matrices of a given size.

(b) Why are the integers not a field? Because not every integer has a multiplicative inverse *that is an integer*. For instance, the multiplicative inverse of 3 is $\frac{1}{3}$, which is not an integer.

(c) Why are the natural numbers not a ring? Because they do not contain an additive identity (although you might see a textbook which includes 0 in the natural numbers). Also, the additive inverses of natural numbers are not natural numbers. For instance, the additive inverse of 3 is -3, which is not a natural number.

(d) Why is the set of all quadratic polynomials not a ring? The set of quadratic polynomials is not closed under multiplication. For instance, if you multiply $x^2 + 1$ by $x^2 - 1$, you obtain $x^4 - 1$, which is not quadratic.

(e) Write the multiplicative inverse of $3 - 2i$ in $a + bi$ form.

$$\frac{1}{3 - 2i} \cdot \frac{3 + 2i}{3 + 2i} = \frac{3 + 2i}{9 - 4i^2} = \frac{3 + 2i}{9 + 4} = \frac{3}{13} + \frac{2}{13}i.$$

(f) Show that the set of 2 by 2 matrices with integer entries forms a non-commutative ring. We will show a few of the properties directly and leave the rest to the reader. To see the closure under addition, we technically should show that the sum

$$\begin{bmatrix} a & b \\ c & d \end{bmatrix} + \begin{bmatrix} a' & b' \\ c' & d' \end{bmatrix} = \begin{bmatrix} a + a' & b + b' \\ c + c' & d + d' \end{bmatrix}$$

is again a two by two matrix of integers. But since the integers are closed under addition, each entry of the new matrix is an integer. Hence the set of 2 by 2 matrices of integers is closed under addition. We will show multiplication as well (in part to remind the reader about how to multiply matrices).

$$\begin{bmatrix} a & b \\ c & d \end{bmatrix} \cdot \begin{bmatrix} a' & b' \\ c' & d' \end{bmatrix} = \begin{bmatrix} aa' + bc' & ab' + bd' \\ ca' + dc' & cb' + dd' \end{bmatrix}$$

Since the set of integers is closed under multiplication and addition, each entry in the product matrix is again an integer. Hence the set of 2 by 2 matrices with integer entries is closed under matrix multiplication.

We now check that matrix addition is commutative. Since

$$\begin{bmatrix} a & b \\ c & d \end{bmatrix} + \begin{bmatrix} a' & b' \\ c' & d' \end{bmatrix} = \begin{bmatrix} a + a' & b + b' \\ c + c' & d + d' \end{bmatrix} = \begin{bmatrix} a' & b' \\ c' & d' \end{bmatrix} + \begin{bmatrix} a & b \\ c & d \end{bmatrix},$$

it certainly follows that matrix addition is commutative.

Most of the other properties involve straightforward checks, under two conditions. First, the additive identity element of this ring is the *zero matrix*, $\begin{bmatrix} 0 & 0 \\ 0 & 0 \end{bmatrix}$, while the multiplicative identity element is the *identity matrix*, $\begin{bmatrix} 1 & 0 \\ 0 & 1 \end{bmatrix}$.

To show that this ring is not commutative, we need to give an example of two matrices that do not commute:

$$\begin{bmatrix} 0 & 1 \\ 0 & 0 \end{bmatrix} \cdot \begin{bmatrix} 0 & 0 \\ 1 & 0 \end{bmatrix} = \begin{bmatrix} 1 & 0 \\ 0 & 0 \end{bmatrix},$$

whereas

$$\begin{bmatrix} 0 & 0 \\ 1 & 0 \end{bmatrix} \cdot \begin{bmatrix} 0 & 1 \\ 0 & 0 \end{bmatrix} = \begin{bmatrix} 0 & 0 \\ 0 & 1 \end{bmatrix}$$

Since these answers are different, then certainly the two matrices $\begin{bmatrix} 0 & 1 \\ 0 & 0 \end{bmatrix}$ and $\begin{bmatrix} 0 & 0 \\ 1 & 0 \end{bmatrix}$ do not commute. Hence the ring of 2 by 2 matrices with integer entries is NOT commutative.

(g) Prove that the set of 2 by 2 invertible matrices with complex number entries is NOT a field. We will show that this set of matrices is not closed under addition. Recall that $1 = 1 + 0i$ is a complex number. We have

$$\begin{bmatrix} 1 & 0 \\ 0 & 1 \end{bmatrix} + \begin{bmatrix} -1 & 0 \\ 0 & -1 \end{bmatrix} = \begin{bmatrix} 0 & 0 \\ 0 & 0 \end{bmatrix},$$

which is clearly not an invertible matrix, even though each matrix summand is invertible. Another reason is that the additive identity, the zero matrix, is not invertible and is therefore not an element of the set of 2 by 2 invertible matrices with complex number entries. Hence the set of 2 by 2 invertible matrices with complex number entries is not a field.

(h) Write the multiplicative inverse of $x + yi$ in $a + bi$ form.

$$\frac{1}{x + yi} \cdot \frac{x - yi}{x - yi} = \frac{x - yi}{x^2 - i^2 y^2} = \frac{x - yi}{x^2 + y^2} = \frac{x}{x^2 + y^2} - \frac{y}{x^2 + y^2} i.$$

(i) What is the smallest field that contains 0 and 1? Since any field must be closed under addition and must contain additive inverses, we know that all positive and negative integers must lie in this field. Moreover, since fields must contain multiplicative inverses of all nonzero elements, we must have the numbers $\frac{1}{2}$, $\frac{1}{3}$, etc. in the field. Then, using closure under addition and multiplication, we can obtain any rational number. It turns out that the rational numbers form a field. Thus, the rational numbers are the smallest field containing zero and one (under usual operations). [If you want to use operations mod 2 ($1+1 = 0$), then you can make a field containing only 0 and 1!]

(j) Using the field properties listed above, prove that $(a + b)c = ac + bc$. We have $(a + b)c = c(a + b) = ca + cb = ac + bc$, where we have used the commutativity of multiplication and the distributive property in the way it was originally stated above.

(k) Let F be the field of rational functions $\dfrac{p(x)}{q(x)}$, where $p(x)$ and $q(x)$ are any polynomials with real coefficients and $q(x) \neq 0$.

    i. Show that F contains a multiplicative identity element. The element $1 = \frac{1}{1}$ is an element of F, because 1 is a (degree zero) polynomial.

    ii. Show that F is closed under multiplication.

$$\frac{p(x)}{q(x)} \cdot \frac{a(x)}{b(x)} = \frac{p(x)a(x)}{q(x)b(x)}$$

Polynomials are closed under multiplication. Since $q(x)$ and $b(x)$ are not 0, then $q(x)b(x) \neq 0$. So the product of two elements of F is another element of F.

iii. Show that F is closed under addition.

$$\frac{p(x)}{q(x)} + \frac{a(x)}{b(x)} = \frac{p(x)b(x) + q(x)a(x)}{q(x)b(x)}$$

Again, since polynomials are closed under multiplication and addition, and since the denominator is not zero, the sum of two elements of F is again an element of F.

iv. Show that every non-zero element of F is invertible. If $\frac{p(x)}{q(x)} \neq 0$, then $p(x) \neq 0$. So that means that $\frac{q(x)}{p(x)}$ is an element of F. Multiplying, we get

$$\frac{p(x)}{q(x)} \cdot \frac{q(x)}{p(x)} = \frac{p(x)q(x)}{p(x)q(x)} = 1.$$

Hence, every non-zero element of F is invertible.

b. Apply basic properties of real and complex numbers in constructing mathematical arguments (e.g., if $a < b$ and $c < 0$, then $ac > bc$)

1. What are some basic properties of real and complex numbers?

   The field properties are the most basic properties of real and complex numbers. In addition, for the real numbers there are properties of ordering, like the Trichotomy Axiom (mentioned below), and the following. Fill in the blanks.

   (a) If $a < b$ and $c < d$, then $a + c$ _____ $b + d$.

   (b) If $a < b$ and $c > 0$, then ac _____ bc.

   (c) If $a < b$ and $c < 0$, then ac _____ bc.

   (d) If $a \leq b$ and $b \leq a$, then a _____ b.

   (e) If $a < b$ and $b < c$, then a _____ c.

   (f) (Trichotomy) If a and b are real numbers, then exactly one of the following is true: $a < b$, $a > b$, or a _____ b.

   ANS: $<, <, >, =, <, =$.

   There are also properties of equality. List as many as you can:

   ANS: Reflexive, Symmetric, and Transitive Properties of Equality, Additive Property of Equality, Multiplicative Property of Equality

2. What is the definition of a rational number? ... of a complex number?

   A rational number can be expressed as the ratio of two integers. So, any rational number can be written as $\frac{p}{q}$, where p and q are integers, and $q \neq 0$.

A complex number can be expressed as the sum of a real number and an imaginary number. So, any complex number can be written as $a+bi$, where a and b are real numbers and $i^2 = -1$. What is an imaginary number?

ANS: An imaginary number is one satisfying $x^2 \leq 0$. [There is sometimes a debate on whether 0 is imaginary or not. I choose to think of 0 as $0i$ in this case, making it imaginary. It's also real. No one said that numbers had to be either real or imaginary, but not both.]

3. Sample Problems

   (a) What is proved by the following?

   Suppose that $\sqrt{2} = \frac{p}{q}$, where $\frac{p}{q}$ is written in lowest terms; i.e., p and q are integers that have no common factors other than 1. Then $2 = \frac{p^2}{q^2}$. Since p and q have no common factors, we must have $q = 1$ or else $\frac{p^2}{q^2}$ would not be an integer. So $q = 1$ and $p^2 = 2$. But this is impossible because there is no integer p with $p^2 = 2$. □

   (b) Show on a number line that if $a > b > 0$, then $-a < -b$.

   (c) Let a and b be integers with $b \neq 0$. Consider the following statement: If $\frac{a}{b} < 1$, then $a < b$.

      i. List some values for a and b that make the statement true.

      ii. List some values for a and b that make the statement false.

      iii. What is a condition on a and/or b that will make the statement necessarily true?

4. Answers to Sample Problems

   (a) What is proved by the following?

   Suppose that $\sqrt{2} = \frac{p}{q}$, where $\frac{p}{q}$ is written in lowest terms; i.e., p and q are integers that have no common factors other than 1. Then $2 = \frac{p^2}{q^2}$. Since p and q have no common factors, we must have $q = 1$ or else $\frac{p^2}{q^2}$ would not be an integer. So $q = 1$ and $p^2 = 2$. But this is impossible because there is no integer p with $p^2 = 2$. □

   This is a proof (by contradiction) that $\sqrt{2}$ is irrational. The proof started by assuming that $\sqrt{2}$ was rational and deduced a contradiction to that assumption. Hence $\sqrt{2}$ must be irrational.

   (b) Show on a number line that if $a > b > 0$, then $-a < -b$. We are told that $a > b > 0$. On a number line, this looks like:

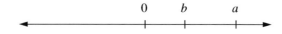

   So, if we put in $-a$ and $-b$ as well, we get:

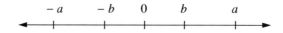

Clearly, $-a$ is to the left of $-b$, and thus $-a < -b$.

(c) Let a and b be integers with $b \neq 0$. Consider the following statement: If $\frac{a}{b} < 1$, then $a < b$.

    i. List some values for a and b that make the statement true. Answers may vary, although b must be greater than zero.

    ii. List some values for a and b that make the statement false. Answers may vary, although b must be less than zero.

    iii. What is a condition on a and/or b that will make the statement necessarily true? If b is positive, then one can use the Multiplicative Property of Inequality to deduce that the statement must be true. Conversely, if $b < 0$, then the statement is false.

c. Demonstrate knowledge that the rational numbers and real numbers can be ordered and that the complex numbers cannot be ordered, but that any polynomial equation with real coefficients can be solved in the complex field

1. What does it mean to be "ordered?"

   A set is "totally ordered" (or just "ordered") if, given any two elements a and b in the set, either $a \leq b$ or $b \leq a$. Notice that because of the Trichotomy Axiom of real numbers, we know that if x and y are real numbers, either (i) $x < y$, (ii) $x > y$, or (iii) $x = y$. Thus, the real numbers, and any subset of the real numbers, is ordered.

2. Why can't the complex numbers be ordered?

   This question is misleading. The complex numbers can indeed be ordered, but not in a meaningful way. We will examine some of the consequences of trying to order the complex numbers in the sample problems.

3. Fundamental Theorem of Algebra

   See **2.2 Polynomial Equations and Inequalities**, section **a** (below) for more information on the Fundamental Theorem of Algebra, which states that if $f(x)$ is a polynomial with real coefficients, then $f(x)$ can be factored into linear and quadratic factors, each of which has real coefficients. Moreover, $f(x)$ can be factored entirely into linear factors if you allow your factors to have complex coefficients.

   [Mathematicians say: Every complex polynomial has a root in $\mathbb{C}$. A fancy way to say this is to say that $\mathbb{C}$ is an "algebraically closed" field.]

4. Sample Problems

   (a) Which of the following sets is an ordered field: complex numbers, rational numbers, integers, or natural numbers?

   (b) List three reasons why the set of 2 by 2 matrices with real number entries do not form an ordered field.

   (c) What is the maximum number of complex solutions to $x^{17} - 573x^9 + 54x^8 - 167x + 2 = 0$?

(d) One way to order the complex numbers is as follows: $(a + bi) \lll (c + di)$ if (1) $a < c$ or (2) $a = c$ and $b < d$. In other words, compare the real parts to determine which is bigger. If they are the same, then move to the imaginary parts.

    i. Which is bigger, 2 or 20?

    ii. Which is bigger, $1 + 2i$ or $1 + 20i$?

    iii. Which is bigger, $2 + i$ or $-100 - 100i$?

    iv. Which is bigger, $100i$ or 1?

    v. What might be a disadvantage to this ordering?

(e) Another way to order the complex numbers is by their magnitudes. The magnitude of $a + bi$ is $\sqrt{a^2 + b^2}$, which is a real number. So, $(a + bi) \lll (c + di)$ if $\sqrt{a^2 + b^2} < \sqrt{c^2 + d^2}$.

    i. Which is bigger, 2 or 20?

    ii. Which is bigger, -2 or -20?

    iii. Which is bigger, 5 or $3 + 4i$?

    iv. Which is bigger, $1 + i$ or $1 - i$?

    v. What might be a disadvantage to this ordering?

5. Answers to Sample Problems

(a) Which of the following sets is an ordered field: complex numbers, rational numbers, integers, or natural numbers? The rational numbers, integers, and natural numbers are all ordered via $<$, because they are subsets of the (ordered) real numbers.

(b) List three reasons why the set of 2 by 2 matrices with real number entries do not form an ordered field. It's certainly hard to order them (in a meaningful way), but the set of 2 by 2 real matrices do not even form a field. Indeed, matrices like $\begin{bmatrix} 1 & 0 \\ 0 & 0 \end{bmatrix}$ do not even have a multiplicative inverse.

(c) What is the maximum number of complex solutions to $x^{17} - 573x^9 + 54x^8 - 167x + 2 = 0$? Seventeen. The only time there may be fewer than 17 complex roots is if some of the roots have a multiplicity greater than one (like double roots, triple roots, etc.).

(d) One way to order the complex numbers is as follows: $(a + bi) \lll (c + di)$ if (1) $a < c$ or (2) $a = c$ and $b < d$. In other words, compare the real parts to determine which is bigger. If they are the same, then move to the imaginary parts.

    i. Which is bigger, 2 or 20? ANS: 20

    ii. Which is bigger, $1 + 2i$ or $1 + 20i$? ANS: $1 + 20i$

    iii. Which is bigger, $2 + i$ or $-100 - 100i$? ANS: $2 + i$

    iv. Which is bigger, $100i$ or 1? ANS: 1

    v. What might be a disadvantage to this ordering? One disadvantage is that complex numbers with large imaginary parts but small real parts might be considered smaller than numbers that have small imaginary parts and only slightly bigger real parts. This method seems to give undue importance to the real part of a complex number.

(e) Another way to order the complex numbers is by their magnitudes. The magnitude of $a+bi$ is $\sqrt{a^2+b^2}$, which is a real number. So, $(a+bi) \lll (c+di)$ if $\sqrt{a^2+b^2} < \sqrt{c^2+d^2}$.

    i. Which is bigger, 2 or 20? ANS: 20

    ii. Which is bigger, -2 or -20? ANS: -20

    iii. Which is bigger, 5 or $3+4i$? ANS: same magnitude

    iv. Which is bigger, $1+i$ or $1-i$? ANS: same magnitude

    v. What might be a disadvantage to this ordering? One disadvantage is that it is not consistent with the ordering of real numbers. ($-20 \ggg -2$, for instance.) Another disadvantage is that sometimes very different-looking complex numbers have the same magnitude. However, even though it may have drawbacks, this way of measuring the "size" of a complex number is very commonly used because it contains useful geometric information.

d. Identify and translate between equivalent forms of algebraic expressions and equations using a variety of techniques (e.g., factoring, applying properties of operations)
e. Justify the steps in manipulating algebraic expressions and solving algebraic equations and inequalities

We will treat these two standards together since they both address the techniques for manipulating expressions, equations, and inequalities, as well as the justifications for those techniques.

1. What are some of the techniques for translating between equivalent expressions? What are the justifications for these techniques?

An expression represents a number. When simplifying an expression (which involves translating between equivalent expressions), we have to make sure that we do not change the number represented by the expression. Here are some techniques which do not change the value of an expression, along with a short description, an example, and a brief justification for each.

- *Gathering like terms.* This can be thought of as a specific type of factoring, below. As an example, $3x - 2x + 4x$ can be rewritten as $5x$. This is justified by the distributive property (in reverse):
$$3x - 2x + 4x = (3 - 2 + 4)x = 5x.$$

- *Multiplying out.* This can be useful on its own or as part of other techniques. For example, when working with complex numbers, one might have the expression $(2 - 3i)(2 + 3i)$, which can be rewritten as $4 - 9i^2$, or 13, when multiplied out. This can also be applied to separating fractions over the same denominator, as in rewriting $\dfrac{x^2 - 5}{x}$ as $\dfrac{x^2}{x} - \dfrac{5}{x}$, or $x - \dfrac{5}{x}$. (We can think of this as distributing $\dfrac{1}{x}$ over the numerator.) This is again justified via the distributive property.

- *Factoring.* In addition to gathering like terms, sometimes factoring can help transform an expression into a more useful format. For instance, $x^2 - 5x + 6$ can be factored as $(x - 2)(x - 3)$, which can tell us what values of x will make the expression equal to 0.

Factoring is also a form of the distributive property (in reverse):

$$\begin{aligned} x^2 - 5x + 6 &= x^2 - 2x - 3x + 6 \\ &= x(x-2) - 3(x-2) \\ &= (x-2)(x-3). \end{aligned}$$

- *Adding 0.* This is often a useful trick. For example, when completing the square on a quadratic expression, we can write $x^2 + 4x - 3$ as $x^2 + 4x + 4 - 4 - 3$, which is also $(x+2)^2 - 7$. Note that we added 0 by adding 4 and subtracting 4. The fact that adding 0 doesn't change the value of a number is because 0 is the additive identity.

- *Multiplying by 1.* This is often useful as well. For example, when rationalizing a denominator, such as $\dfrac{1}{2 + \sqrt{5}}$, we often multiply by a suitable form of 1.

$$\left(\frac{1}{2 + \sqrt{5}} \right) \left(\frac{2 - \sqrt{5}}{2 - \sqrt{5}} \right) \quad \text{which is also} \quad \frac{2 - \sqrt{5}}{4 - 5} \quad \text{or} \quad \sqrt{5} - 2.$$

  This technique is also often used to get a common denominator between two rational expressions. The fact that multiplying by 1 doesn't change the value of a number is because 1 is the multiplicative identity.

- *Canceling common factors in a rational expression.* This is essentially reducing a rational expression to its lowest terms. For instance, $\dfrac{2x^2 - 16x}{4x^3}$ can be reduced to $\dfrac{x-8}{2x^2}$ by canceling the common factor of $2x$ that appears in the numerator and denominator. This can be justified by unraveling the meaning of a rational number. There are many equivalent forms of a rational number (like $\frac{1}{2}, \frac{2}{4}, \frac{3}{6}$, etc.) and so we are interested in the form that is in lowest terms (or at least lower terms).

  WARNING! There is a caveat here in that there can be a subtle difference between the simplified version and the original version in terms of the domain of acceptable values for x. In the above example, neither expression is defined when $x = 0$, so the second expression is equivalent to the first. However, if we write $\dfrac{(x-2)(x-3)}{x-2}$ as $x - 3$, then we have exchanged an expression where x cannot equal 2 for an expression in which x could equal 2. The expressions are equivalent, provided $x \neq 2$.

2. What are some of the techniques for translating between equivalent equations?

   An equation is a statement that two expressions denote the same number. Because we have two expressions, we have more techniques available to transform to equivalent equations. In addition to the above techniques for transforming each expression in the equation, we can also utilize the following. As before, each will be briefly explained, along with an example. Justifications will come later.

   - *Performing the same invertible (i.e. reversible) operation to both sides.* There are a variety of operations that are reversible: addition (or subtraction) of any number, multiplication (or division) by any non-zero number, extracting roots of both sides. If we are dealing with real numbers, then raising both sides to an odd power is reversible. Also, we can exponentiate both sides as powers of the same base b ($b > 0, b \neq 1$). This includes techniques like clearing denominators or raising a base to both sides of the equation, techniques which can not be done with expressions alone because they would change the value of the original expression. For example, to solve $\frac{1}{x} + 2 = \frac{5}{x}$, one can multiply both sides of the equation by x (provided $x \neq 0$ – see non-invertible operations, below) to obtain $1 + 2x = 5$, or $x = 2$. Likewise, to solve $\log x = 3$, we can transform to $10^{\log x} = 10^3$, or $x = 1000$.

- *Performing the same non-invertible (i.e. non-reversible) operation to both sides.* Here, we can still transform the equation into a new equation, but we might lose information along the way, and we might introduce new solutions that are not solutions of the original equation, called *extraneous* solutions. We have to know that when multiplying (or dividing) by a variable that might equal zero, or by raising both sides to an even power (like squaring), that we might introduce extraneous solutions. This is just further reason always to check your answers. Let's look at some examples.

  First, consider $\frac{2}{x} = 3$. We can solve this equation by multiplying both sides by x to obtain $2 = 3x$. Now we divide both sides by 3 (or multiply both sides by $\frac{1}{3}$) to get $x = \frac{2}{3}$. We check this in the original equation: $\frac{2}{\frac{2}{3}} = 2 \cdot \frac{3}{2} = 3$, which is correct.

  Second, let's try $\sqrt{x - 5} = 6$. Squaring both sides, we obtain $x - 5 = 36$ and so $x = 41$. Checking this is the original equation, we get $\sqrt{41 - 5} = \sqrt{36} = 6$.

  Note that we did not obtain any extraneous solutions in the first two examples because we checked our answers and they satisfied the original equations.

3. Why do extraneous solutions arise?

   Extraneous solutions can arise whenever your algebraic step is not reversible. For instance, $4 = -4$ is a FALSE equation, but the transformed equation from squaring both sides ($16 = 16$) is true. That's essentially how extraneous solutions can arise. Squaring both sides of an equation is not a reversible step. Neither is multiplying both sides by zero. One normally wouldn't multiply both sides of an equation by zero on purpose, but when variables are involved, students sometimes forget to check if they have inadvertently introduced extraneous solutions.

4. What are some examples of extraneous solutions?

   Let's do some examples in which extraneous solutions arise. First, consider the equation $\sqrt{4 - 3x^2} = x$. Squaring both sides, we get $4 - 3x^2 = x^2$, which simplifies to $4 = 4x^2$ or $x^2 = 1$. There are two solutions: $x = 1$ or $x = -1$ (often written $x = \pm 1$).

   If we check these values in the original equation, it's clear that $x = 1$ is a valid solution, but $x = -1$ is extraneous:

   $$\sqrt{4 - 3(-1)^2} = \sqrt{4 - 3} = \sqrt{1} = 1 \neq -1.$$

   Squaring both sides of the original equation introduced an extraneous solution.

As a second example, consider $\dfrac{2x}{x-2} = 3 + \dfrac{4}{x-2}$. To clear the denominators, we will multiply both sides by $x - 2$. So we get

$$
\begin{aligned}
2x &= 3(x-2) + 4 \\
2x &= 3x - 6 + 4 \\
2x &= 3x - 2 \\
2 &= x.
\end{aligned}
$$

So $x = 2$. But if we try to check this value in the original equation, we get a denominator of zero. So $x = 2$ is an extraneous solution and there is no solution to the original equation. Here, we introduced the extraneous solution when we multiplied both sides by $x - 2$. This step is only reversible if $x - 2 \neq 0$, i.e., if $x \neq 2$. If $x = 2$, it can sometimes still be done, but it destroys your chances of finding any other solutions. It's like trying to solve $x + 1 = 2$ by multiplying both sides by zero. You just get $0 = 0$, which is true, but you have lost any other information from the original equation.

5. What are some of the techniques for translating between equivalent inequalities?

   An inequality is a statement that compares two expressions, and says that one is larger than (or larger than or equal to) the other. Again, we can transform any expression into an equivalent expression using the above rules. We can also transform both sides of an inequality by adding or subtracting the same number from both sides. We can also multiply or divide by a positive number without changing the direction of the inequality. But when we multiply or divide both sides of an inequality by a negative number, then we need to reverse the direction of the inequality sign. These properties can be found in section **b** above.

6. What are the justifications for these techniques?

   Solving equations and inequalities with variables is what most people think of when they think of algebra. There are rules to how equations and inequalities can be manipulated, and students sometimes focus too much on the rules and lose sight of why the rules are true.

   When working with equalities, most algebraic steps are based on what it means for two things to be exactly the same. If you think of numbers, a number can only equal itself - it cannot equal a different number. So $4 = 4$ is true, but $4 = 2$ is false. If two things are equal to begin with, and we transform both things in the exact same way, then the two transformed things must still be equal. This is clear. If you start with a true equality, like $4 = 4$, and you add ten to both sides, then the result (i.e. $14 = 14$) must still be a true equality. That explains the vast majority of algebraic manipulations of equations.

   Inequalities are similar, but there are some transformations that will change the direction of the inequality (namely, multiplying or dividing by a negative number), and so one must be careful. If you start with a true inequality, like $4 > 2$, and you subtract 10 from both sides, you still get a true inequality: $-6 > -8$. But if you now multiply both sides of this inequality by -1, then you must remember to change the direction of the inequality. Namely, $-6 > -8$, but $6 < 8$. (This can be visualized on a number line. See Sample Problems in section **b** above.

Understanding that we are simply maintaining relationships of equality or inequality through-out the algebraic steps will help students understand why algebra leads toward a correct solution.

7. Sample Problems

   (a) Solve the following equations and inequalities. Identify any extraneous solutions, if they arise.

        i. $2x - 5 = 16$.

       ii. $2x - 5 > 16$.

      iii. $bx - c = 16$.

      iv. $\dfrac{x}{x-2} = 2$.

       v. $\dfrac{x}{x-1} = M$.

      vi. $\dfrac{x}{x-2} \leq 2$. (Careful!)

     vii. $\dfrac{x}{x+3} = 3 - \dfrac{3}{x+3}$.

    viii. $\sqrt{x} + \sqrt{x+3} = 3$.

     ix. $\sqrt{x^2 + 2x + 1} = x + 1$ (Careful!)

   (b) Explain why the solution to $3x - 5 = 4$ is $x = 3$ by showing each step. List all the properties you use.

   (c) Explain why the solution to $-3x - 5 < 4$ is $x > -3$ by showing each step. List all the properties you use.

   (d) Using various ring properties and properties of equality, give reasons for the proof of the Multiplication Property of Zero: If x is in a ring, then $0x = 0$.

   - $0 + 0 = 0$
   - $(0 + 0)x = 0x$
   - $0x + 0x = 0x$
   - $0x + 0x = 0x + 0$
   - $0x = 0$.

8. Answers to Sample Problems

   (a) Solve the following equations and inequalities. Identify any extraneous solutions, if they arise.

        i. $2x - 5 = 16$. $x = \dfrac{21}{2} = 10.5$

       ii. $2x - 5 > 16$. $x > \dfrac{21}{2} = 10.5$

      iii. $bx - c = 16$. $x = \dfrac{16 + c}{b}$, assuming $b \neq 0$.

      iv. $\dfrac{x}{x-2} = 2$. $x = 4$

v. $\dfrac{x}{x-1} = M$. $x = \dfrac{M}{M-1}$, assuming $M \neq 1$.
Here's one solution:

$$
\begin{aligned}
\frac{x}{x-1} &= M \\
x &= M(x-1) = Mx - M \\
x - Mx &= -M \\
x(1-M) &= -M \\
x &= \frac{-M}{1-M} = \frac{M}{M-1}.
\end{aligned}
$$

vi. $\dfrac{x}{x-2} \leq 2$. (Careful!) $x \geq 4$ or $x < 2$.
To see this, let's rewrite the left hand side by finding quotient and remainder polynomials first. It will simplify things a little bit by getting the variable x in only one location.

$$ 2 \geq \frac{x}{x-2} = \frac{x-2+2}{x-2} = 1 + \frac{2}{x-2}, $$

and so $1 \geq \frac{2}{x-2}$. Now we need to multiply by $x-2$ but whether or not we change the direction of the inequality depends on the value of x. So let's look at two cases: $x - 2 < 0$ (i.e., $x < 2$) and $x - 2 > 0$ (i.e., $x > 2$). (Notice that if $x = 2$ we have an undefined fraction.)
Case 1: $x - 2 < 0$. Multiplying by $x - 2$, we get $x - 2 \leq 2$. Since $x - 2$ is negative in this case, it is certainly less than 2. Every value of x in this case solves the inequality.
Case 2: $x - 2 > 0$. Multiplying by $x - 2$, we get $x - 2 \geq 2$, or $x \geq 4$. So not every value of x in this case will work. We also have to restrict x to be at least 4.
Putting the two cases together, we get that $x < 2$ or $x \geq 4$.

vii. $\dfrac{x}{x+3} = 3 - \dfrac{3}{x+3}$. The "solution" $x = -3$ is extraneous; there are no solutions.

viii. $\sqrt{x} + \sqrt{x+3} = 3$. $x = 1$

ix. $\sqrt{x^2 + 2x + 1} = x + 1$ (Careful!) This looks like an identity once you square both sides. It is tempting to state that the equation is true for all values of x. But it's not. Try $x = -2$ for instance. $\sqrt{4 - 4 + 1} = 1 \neq -2 + 1$. The equation is only true if the right-hand side is not negative. That is, $x + 1 \geq 0$, or $x \geq -1$. To reiterate: this equation is true for all values of x that are greater than or equal to -1.

(b) Explain why the solution to $3x - 5 = 4$ is $x = 3$ by showing each step. List all the properties you use.

A quick word about the following list. Each stated reason is explaining the algebraic reasoning behind the transition from the previous line to the current line. So, in the third step, "Arithmetic" refers to the transition from $4 + 5$ to 9 on the right hand side. It does not refer to the equation $(3x - 5) + 5 = 9$. The only exception to this pattern is the first "Given."

$$
\begin{array}{ll}
3x - 5 = 4 & \text{Given} \\
(3x - 5) + 5 = 4 + 5 & \text{Additive Property of Equality} \\
(3x - 5) + 5 = 9 & \text{Arithmetic} \\
(3x + (-5)) + 5 = 9 & \text{Definition of Subtraction} \\
3x + ((-5) + 5) = 9 & \text{Associative Property of Addition} \\
3x + 0 = 9 & \text{Additive Inverse} \\
3x = 9 & \text{Additive Identity} \\
\frac{1}{3}(3x) = \frac{1}{3}(9) & \text{Multiplicative Property of Equality} \\
\frac{1}{3}(3x) = 3 & \text{Arithmetic} \\
\left(\frac{1}{3} \cdot 3\right) x = 3 & \text{Associative Property of Multiplication} \\
1x = 3 & \text{Multiplicative Inverse} \\
x = 3 & \text{Multiplicative Identity}
\end{array}
$$

(c) Explain why the solution to $-3x - 5 < 4$ is $x > -3$ by showing each step. List all the properties you use.

$$
\begin{array}{ll}
-3x - 5 < 4 & \text{Given} \\
(-3x - 5) + 5 < 4 + 5 & \text{Additive Property of Inequality} \\
(-3x - 5) + 5 < 9 & \text{Arithmetic} \\
(-3x + (-5)) + 5 < 9 & \text{Definition of Subtraction} \\
-3x + ((-5) + 5) < 9 & \text{Associative Property of Addition} \\
-3x + 0 < 9 & \text{Additive Inverse} \\
-3x < 9 & \text{Additive Identity} \\
-\frac{1}{3}(-3x) > -\frac{1}{3}(9) & \text{Multiplicative Property of Inequality} \\
-\frac{1}{3}(-3x) > -3 & \text{Arithmetic} \\
\left(-\frac{1}{3} \cdot -3\right) x > -3 & \text{Associative Property of Multiplication} \\
1x > -3 & \text{Multiplicative Inverse} \\
x > -3 & \text{Multiplicative Identity}
\end{array}
$$

(d) Using various ring properties and properties of equality, give reasons for the proof of the Multiplication Property of Zero: If x is in a ring, then $0x = 0$.

- $0 + 0 = 0$ Additive Identity (anything plus 0 equals itself)
- $(0 + 0)x = 0x$ Multiplicative Property of Equality (i.e., multiply both sides by x)
- $0x + 0x = 0x$ Distributive Property

- $0x + 0x = 0x + 0$ Additive Identity
- $0x = 0$.   Additive Property of Equality (in reverse) (i.e., cancel $0x$ from both sides)

f. Represent situations and solve problems using algebraic equations and inequalities

See sections **1.1.c** and **2.3.f** for theoretical underpinnings and practical examples.

2.2 Polynomial Equations and Inequalities

a. Analyze and solve polynomial equations with real coefficients using:

- **the Fundamental Theorem of Algebra**

- **the Rational Root Theorem for polynomials with integer coefficients**

- **the Conjugate Roots Theorem for polynomial equations with real coefficients**

- **the Binomial Theorem**

1. What is the Fundamental Theorem of Algebra?

   The Fundamental Theorem of Algebra says that if $f(x)$ is a polynomial with real coefficients, then $f(x)$ can be factored into linear and quadratic factors, each of which has real coefficients. Moreover, $f(x)$ can be factored entirely into linear factors if you allow your factors to have complex coefficients.

2. How do you use the Fundamental Theorem of Algebra to analyze polynomial equations?

   The main way to use the Fundamental Theorem of Algebra is when determining the number of roots a polynomial has. For example, a polynomial of degree n has at most n roots. Combined with the the following theorems, we can often say more.

   Example: Say f has real coefficients and degree 5. If $2 - i$ is a root of f, then how many real roots can f have? The answer is that f has either one or three real roots. The reason for this is that because f has real coefficients, the Conjugate Roots Theorem says that $2 + i$ is also a root. This accounts for 2 of the roots of f, leaving 3 more complex roots, some of which might (also) be real. Since the complex nonreal roots have to come in conjugate pairs, there are either zero or two more complex nonreal roots. Hence the number of real roots must be three or one. (This includes the multiplicity of a double or triple root, which would count as two or three roots, respectively.)

3. What is the Rational Root Theorem for polynomials with integer coefficients?

   If $f(x) = a_n x^n + a_{n-1} x^{n-1} + \ldots + a_1 x + a_0$, with each a_i an integer, then the Rational Root Theorem says that the only possible rational roots are of the form $\pm \frac{p}{q}$, where p is a divisor of a_0 and q is a divisor of a_n.

   Proof: Suppose $\frac{p}{q}$ is a root of f. Then

   $$0 = f(p/q) = a_n(p/q)^n + a_{n-1}(p/q)^{n-1} + \ldots + a_1(p/q) + a_0.$$

   Multiply by q^n to clear denominators. Then

   $$0 = a_n p^n + a_{n-1} p^{n-1} q + \ldots + a_1 p q^{n-1} + a_0 q^n.$$

   So $-a_0 q^n = a_n p^n + a_{n-1} p^{n-1} q + \ldots + a_1 p q^{n-1} = p(a_n p^{n-1} + a_{n-1} p^{n-2} q + \ldots + a_1 q^{n-1})$, which is clearly divisible by p. If we assume that $\frac{p}{q}$ is in lowest terms, then p has no factors in common with q^n. So p must be a divisor of a_0. Similarly, $-a_n p^n = q(a_{n-1}p^{n-1}+\ldots+a_1 pq^{n-2}+a_0 q^{n-1})$, which is divisible by q. Thus, a_n must be divisible by q. □

Alternate Explanation: Factor $f(x)$ into factors with integer coefficients. If $\pm\frac{p}{q}$ is a root, then $(qx \mp p)$ is a factor. [See Factor Theorem, below.] So, when you multiply out all the factors, q will be a factor of the leading coefficient, a_n, and p will be a factor of the constant term, a_0. [To check this, try multiplying $(2x-3)$ by any polynomial with integer coefficients. Then notice that the leading term is divisible by 2 and the constant term is divisible by 3.]

Example: List all possible rational roots of $g(x) = 2x^3 + 9x^2 + 7x - 6$.

ANS: Any rational root must be a factor of 6 divided by a factor of 2. The possibilities are: $\pm 1, \pm 2, \pm 3, \pm 6, \pm\frac{1}{2}, \pm\frac{3}{2}$.

4. What is the Conjugate Roots Theorem for polynomial equations with real coefficients?

If $f(x)$ is a polynomial with *real* coefficients, and if $f(a+bi)=0$, then the Conjugate Roots Theorem says that $f(a-bi)=0$.

Proof: Since $f(x)$ has real coefficients, $f(x) = \overline{f}(x)$, where $\overline{f}(x)$ is the polynomial obtained by taking the complex conjugate of every coefficient of f. So

$$0 = f(a+bi) = \overline{f(a+bi)} = \overline{f}(\overline{a+bi}) = f(\overline{a+bi}) = f(a-bi). \quad \square$$

Example: Factor $g(x) = x^4 - 5x^3 + 9x^2 - 5x$ if you know that $g(2+i)=0$.

ANS: Since $2+i$ is a root, the Conjugate Roots Theorem says that $2-i$ is also a root. This means that $(x-(2+i))$ and $(x-(2-i))$ are factors of $g(x)$. So

$$\begin{aligned}(x-(2+i))(x-(2-i)) &= x^2 - (2+i)x - (2-i)x + (2+i)(2-i)\\ &= x^2 - 4x + 5\end{aligned}$$

is also a factor of $g(x)$. Notice that x is a factor as well. So, using long division, (or trial and error, or noticing that 1 is a root), we obtain

$$g(x) = x^4 - 5x^3 + 9x^2 - 5x = x(x-1)(x^2 - 4x + 5).$$

5. What is the Conjugate Roots Theorem for polynomial equations with rational coefficients?

If $f(x)$ is a polynomial with *rational* coefficients, and if $f(a+b\sqrt{n})=0$ (with $\sqrt{n}$ irrational), then the Conjugate Roots Theorem says that $f(a-b\sqrt{n})=0$.

Proof: Abstract Algebra. Since f has rational coefficients, f doesn't change when you switch the irrational $\sqrt{n}$ with $-\sqrt{n}$. The proof then is similar to the one using complex conjugation, given above.

Example: Suppose $f(x)$ is quadratic with $f(5-\sqrt{5})=0$. Find a possible formula for $f(x)$.

ANS: Let's find such an f with rational coefficients, which means that we can require $f(5+\sqrt{5})=0$ also. The simplest quadratic is thus

$$\begin{aligned}f(x) &= (x-(5-\sqrt{5}))(x-(5+\sqrt{5}))\\ &= x^2 - (5-\sqrt{5})x - (5+\sqrt{5})x + (5-\sqrt{5})(5+\sqrt{5})\\ &= x^2 - 10x + 20.\end{aligned}$$

6. What is the Binomial Theorem?

$$(x+y)^n = \sum_{k=0}^{n} \binom{n}{k} x^{n-k} y^k,$$

where $\binom{n}{k} = \dfrac{n!}{k!(n-k)!}$ and is read "n choose k." It is also the number of ways to choose k objects from a set of n objects.

The Binomial Theorem can be proved by mathematical induction.

Proof: We start by checking that the formula is true for $n = 1$.

$$\sum_{k=0}^{1} \binom{1}{k} x^{1-k} y^k = \binom{1}{0} x^1 y^0 + \binom{1}{1} x^0 y^1 = 1x + 1y = (x+y)^1.$$

Now we show that whenever the formula is true for some value of n then it is also true for $n+1$. (Via induction, this will imply that the formula is true for any value of n.)

$$\begin{aligned}
(x+y)^{n+1} &= (x+y)(x+y)^n \\
&= (x+y)\left(\sum_{k=0}^{n} \binom{n}{k} x^{n-k} y^k\right) \\
&= \sum_{k=0}^{n} \binom{n}{k} x^{n-k+1} y^k + \sum_{k=0}^{n} \binom{n}{k} x^{n-k} y^{k+1}
\end{aligned}$$

We need to re-index the second summation in order to combine like terms correctly. Let $\ell = k+1$ so that the summation is from $\ell = 1$ to $\ell = n+1$. Then

$$(x+y)^{n+1} = \sum_{k=0}^{n} \binom{n}{k} x^{n-k+1} y^k + \sum_{\ell=1}^{n+1} \binom{n}{\ell-1} x^{n-(\ell-1)} y^\ell$$

Notice that we can combine the middle terms ($1 \le k, \ell \le n$) and notice that we have like terms now, if we match up k in the first sum with ℓ in the second, but that the first and last terms need to be separated out.

$$\begin{aligned}
(x+y)^{n+1} &= x^{n+1} + \left(\sum_{k=1}^{n} \left[\binom{n}{k} + \binom{n}{k-1}\right] x^{n-k+1} y^k\right) + y^{n+1} \\
&= \sum_{k=0}^{n+1} \binom{n+1}{k} x^{n+1-k} y^k,
\end{aligned}$$

which is exactly what we wanted to show. $\square$

Notice that we used an identity of the binomial coefficients, namely

$$\binom{n}{k} + \binom{n}{k-1} = \binom{n+1}{k}.$$

You can verify this identity in the Sample Problems.

Example: Expand $(x+2)^5$.

$$(x+2)^5 = \sum_{k=0}^{5} \binom{5}{k} x^{5-k} 2^k$$

$$= \binom{5}{0} x^5 2^0 + \binom{5}{1} x^4 2^1 + \ldots + \binom{5}{5} x^0 2^5$$

$$= x^5 + 5x^4(2) + 10x^3(4) + 10x^2(8) + 5x(16) + 1(32)$$

$$= x^5 + 10x^4 + 40x^3 + 80x^2 + 80x + 32.$$

7. Sample Problems

    (a) Let $2x^4 - x^3 - 20x^2 + 13x + 30 = 0$.

        i. List all possible rational roots.

        ii. Find all rational roots.

        iii. Find all roots.

    (b) Let $6x^4 + 7x^3 + 6x^2 - 1 = 0$.

        i. List all possible rational roots.

        ii. Find all rational roots.

        iii. Find all roots.

    (c) Factor $x^3 - x - 6$ if you know that one root is $-1 + i\sqrt{2}$.

    (d) Find the coefficient of x^4 in $(x-3)^6$.

    (e) Find the fifth term in the expansion of $(2x - y)^9$.

    (f) Explain why the number of ways to choose k objects from a group of n is the same as the number of ways to choose $n - k$ objects from a group of n.

    (g) Suppose $f(x)$ is a quartic polynomial with integer coefficients. If $f(1 + i) = 0$ and $f(2 - \sqrt{3}) = 0$, then find a possible formula for $f(x)$.

    (h) How many real roots can $x^5 - 3x^2 + x + 1$ have? Be specific.

    (i) Find a possible formula for a polynomial $f(x)$ that satisfies: $f(-2) = f(3) = f(5) = 0$ and $f(0) = 15$.

    (j) If $x^2 - 5x + 6$ is a divisor of the polynomial $f(x)$, then what is the minimum degree of f? What is $f(2)$? What is $f(3)$? Suppose $f(4) = 0$. Find a formula for $f(x)$.

    (k) Verify that $\binom{n}{k} + \binom{n}{k-1} = \binom{n+1}{k}$.

8. Answers to Sample Problems

    (a) Let $2x^4 - x^3 - 20x^2 + 13x + 30 = 0$.

        i. List all possible rational roots. $\pm 1, \pm 2, \pm 3, \pm 5, \pm 6, \pm 10, \pm 15, \pm 30, \pm\frac{1}{2}, \pm\frac{3}{2}, \pm\frac{5}{2}, \pm\frac{15}{2}$.

    ii. Find all rational roots.

$$2x^4 - x^3 - 20x^2 + 13x + 30 = (x+1)(2x^3 - 3x^2 - 17x + 30) = (x+1)(x-2)(x+3)(2x-5)$$

    So, the rational roots are $-1, 2, -3, \frac{5}{2}$.

    iii. Find all roots. $-1, 2, -3, \frac{5}{2}$. We know the list is complete because the polynomial has degree 4.

(b) Let $6x^4 + 7x^3 + 6x^2 - 1 = 0$.

    i. List all possible rational roots. $\pm 1, \pm \frac{1}{2}, \pm \frac{1}{3}, \pm \frac{1}{6}$.

    ii. Find all rational roots.

$$6x^4 + 7x^3 + 6x^2 - 1 = (2x+1)(3x-1)(x^2 + x + 1)$$

    So, the rational roots are $-\frac{1}{2}$ and $\frac{1}{3}$.

    iii. Find all roots. $-\frac{1}{2}, \frac{1}{3}, \frac{-1 \pm i\sqrt{3}}{2}$. The other roots can be found by completing the square or the Quadratic Formula. (See the next section.)

(c) Factor $x^3 - x - 6$ if you know that one root is $-1 + i\sqrt{2}$. Since the coefficients are real, we know that another root is $-1 - i\sqrt{2}$. Hence

$$(x - (-1 + i\sqrt{2}))(x - (-1 - i\sqrt{2})) = (x + 1 - i\sqrt{2})(x + 1 + i\sqrt{2}) = (x+1)^2 + 2 = x^2 + 2x + 3$$

is a factor of $x^3 - x - 6$. So $x^3 - x - 6 = (x^2 + 2x + 3)(x - 2)$ by long division, or by guess and check, or by looking at the leading coefficient and constant term and deducing the linear factor.

(d) Find the coefficient of x^4 in $(x - 3)^6$. 135. The $k = 2$ term is:

$$\binom{6}{2} x^{6-2}(-3)^2 = 15x^4(9) = 135x^4.$$

(e) Find the fifth term in the expansion of $(2x - y)^9$. The first term corresponds to $k = 0$ in the summation. So the fifth term corresponds to $k = 4$.

$$\binom{9}{4}(2x)^5(-y)^4 = \frac{(9)(8)(7)(6)(5!)}{(4)(3)(2)(1)(5!)}(32x^5)(y^4) = 4032x^5y^4.$$

(f) Explain why the number of ways to choose k objects from a group of n is the same as the number of ways to choose $n - k$ objects from a group of n. If you choose k objects to include in your subgroup, then you could also think of that as simultaneously choosing $n - k$ objects to exclude from your subgroup. Each way to choose a few is also a way to exclude all the rest. Mathematically, this means $\binom{n}{k} = \binom{n}{n-k}$.

(g) Suppose $f(x)$ is a quartic polynomial with integer coefficients. If $f(1 + i) = 0$ and $f(2 - \sqrt{3}) = 0$, then find a possible formula for $f(x)$. Since f has rational coefficients, we can employ both forms of the Conjugate Roots Theorem, implying that f has four roots. One possible formula for f is thus:

$$f(x) = (x - (1 + i))(x - (1 - i))(x - (2 - \sqrt{3}))(x - (2 + \sqrt{3})),$$

which equals $(x^2 - 2x + 2)(x^2 - 4x + 1) = x^4 - 6x^3 + 11x^2 - 10x + 2$.

(h) How many real roots can $x^5 - 3x^2 + x + 1$ have? Be specific. This polynomial could have 1, 3, or 5 real roots. However, we can use synthetic substitution (or long division) to see that 1 is a double root. Thus the polynomial must have 3 or 5 real roots.

(i) Find a possible formula for a polynomial $f(x)$ that satisfies: $f(-2) = f(3) = f(5) = 0$ and $f(0) = 15$. We know that f must have factors $(x + 2)$, $(x - 3)$, and $(x - 5)$. So we could guess $f(x) = (x + 2)(x - 3)(x - 5)$, but this satisfies $f(0) = 30$, which is not what we want. So, we could multiply our guess by $\frac{1}{2}$, which doesn't change the roots. Thus a correct answer is

$$f(x) = \frac{1}{2}(x + 2)(x - 3)(x - 5) = \frac{1}{2}(x^3 - 6x^2 - x + 30) = \frac{1}{2}x^3 - 3x^2 - \frac{1}{2}x + 15.$$

(j) If $x^2 - 5x + 6$ is a divisor of the polynomial $f(x)$, then what is the minimum degree of f? What is $f(2)$? What is $f(3)$? Suppose $f(4) = 0$. Find a formula for $f(x)$. The minimum degree of f would be 2. Since $2^2 - 5(2) + 6 = 0$, $f(2) = 0$. Similarly, $f(3) = 0$. If we also know that $f(4) = 0$, then f must have a factor of $(x - 4)$ as well, bringing its minimum degree up to 3. One possible formula for $f(x)$ is

$$(x^2 - 5x + 6)(x - 4) = x^3 - 9x^2 + 26x - 24.$$

(k) Verify that $\dbinom{n}{k} + \dbinom{n}{k-1} = \dbinom{n+1}{k}$. We will write out the choose functions and then get a common denominator.

$$
\begin{aligned}
\binom{n}{k} + \binom{n}{k-1} &= \frac{n!}{k!(n-k)!} + \frac{n!}{(k-1)!(n-(k-1))!} \\
&= \frac{n!(n-k+1)}{k!(n-k)!(n-k+1)} + \frac{n!(k)}{(k-1)!(n-k+1)!(k)} \\
&= \frac{n!(n-k+1) + n!(k)}{k!(n-k+1)!} \\
&= \frac{n!(n+1)}{k!(n+1-k)!} = \frac{(n+1)!}{k!(n+1-k)!} = \binom{n+1}{k}
\end{aligned}
$$

Another way to justify it is using counting and the choice function. Let's say that there are $n + 1$ people in a group, and you are one of them. Suppose they need a committee of k people from this group. There are $\dbinom{n+1}{k}$ ways to choose that committee.

Now let's count the same number of committees, but let's consider if you are on the committee or not. How many committees are you on? Well, since you are one of the people, there are only n people left in the group, and there are only $k - 1$ seats left on the committee. So there are $\dbinom{n}{k-1}$ committees that have you as a member. How many committees do not have you on them? Well, if you are not on the committee, then there are n people left in the group, and k seats left on the committee. So there are $\dbinom{n}{k}$ committees that you are not on. Adding these two together gives the total number of committees.

b. Prove and use the Factor Theorem and the quadratic formula for real and complex quadratic polynomials

1. What is the Factor Theorem? How do you prove it?

   The Factor Theorem says that $(x - b)$ is a factor of $f(x)$ if and only if $f(b) = 0$.

   Proof: The Factor Theorem is just a special case of the Remainder Theorem, which says that if $f(x)$ is divided by $(x - b)$, then the remainder is $f(b)$. To see this, recall that if you divide $f(x)$ by $(x - b)$, you get a quotient polynomial $q(x)$ and a remainder polynomial $r(x)$ with the degree of $r(x)$ smaller than the degree of $(x - b)$. So $r(x)$ must be a constant, say r. Hence we have

   $$f(x) = (x - b)q(x) + r.$$

   Letting $x = b$ gives the Remainder Theorem: $f(b) = r$. Therefore, $f(b) = 0$ if and only if the remainder is zero, i.e., exactly when $(x - b)$ is a factor of $f(x)$.   □

   Example: Find the roots of $f(x) = x^5 + 8x^4 + 19x^3 + 8x^2 - 20x - 16$.

   ANS: Using the Remainder Theorem (and synthetic substitution), we notice that both 1 and -1 are roots, which shortens the calculations:

x	1	8	19	8	-20	-16	
1	1	9	28	36	16	0	root
-1	1	8	20	16	0		root
-1	1	7	13	3			(not a double root)
-2	1	6	8	0			root
-2	1	4	0				double root
-4	1	0					root

   (You can also try plugging in 1, -1, -2, and -4 into the polynomial to obtain zero. Review synthetic substitution if you wish to use it.) The roots are : 1, -1, -2, and -4, where -2 is a double root. This also means that

   $$f(x) = x^5 + 8x^4 + 19x^3 + 8x^2 - 20x - 16 = (x - 1)(x + 1)(x + 2)^2(x + 4).$$

2. What is the Quadratic Formula for real and complex quadratic polynomials?

   If $ax^2 + bx + c = 0$ with $a \neq 0$, then $x = \dfrac{-b \pm \sqrt{b^2 - 4ac}}{2a}$.

   This formula will be derived as a sample problem. A Cubic Formula and a Quartic Formula also exist, but there is no Quintic Formula!

3. Sample Problems

   (a) Solve the following quadratic equations.

       i. $2x^2 = 20$.

       ii. $3(x + 4)^2 = 12$.

       iii. $x^2 - 6 = 5x$.

       iv. $x^2 + 6 = 5x$.

  v. $x^2 + 6x = 5$.

  vi. $3x^2 + 6x = 5$.

(b) Use the quadratic formula to solve the following. Leave constants in your answer, if necessary. If the answers are complex, write them in $a + b\mathbf{i}$ form.

  i. $x^2 + bx + 1 = 0$.

  ii. $x^2 - x + 1 = 0$.

  iii. $-\dfrac{1}{2}At^2 + Vt + S = 0$.

(c) Let $f(x) = x^2 - bx + (b - 1)$. Find $f(1)$. Explain how the Factor Theorem allows you to factor $f(x)$. Then, factor $f(x)$.

(d) Show that in $x^2 + bx + c = 0$, the sum of the two roots is $-b$ and the product of the two roots is c.

(e) Solve $z^2 - \mathbf{i}z + 2 = 0$.

(f) Solve $x^2 + 3x = -5$.

(g) Derive the Quadratic Formula. [Hint: Complete the Square.]

4. **Answers to Sample Problems**

(a) Solve the following quadratic equations.

  i. $2x^2 = 20$. $x = \pm\sqrt{10}$ (I used inspection.)

  ii. $3(x + 4)^2 = 12$. $x = -4 \pm 2$, i.e. $x = -2$ or $x = -6$. (I used inspection.)

  iii. $x^2 - 6 = 5x$. $x = 6$ or $x = -1$. (I factored.)

  iv. $x^2 + 6 = 5x$. $x = 2$ or $x = 3$. (I factored.)

  v. $x^2 + 6x = 5$. $x = -3 \pm \sqrt{14}$. (I completed the square.)

  vi. $3x^2 + 6x = 5$. $x = -1 \pm \sqrt{\frac{8}{3}}$. (I completed the square.)

(b) Use the quadratic formula to solve the following. Leave constants in your answer, if necessary. If the answers are complex, write them in $a + b\mathbf{i}$ form.

  i. $x^2 + bx + 1 = 0$. $x = \dfrac{-b \pm \sqrt{b^2 - 4}}{2}$

  ii. $x^2 - x + 1 = 0$. $x = \dfrac{1 \pm \sqrt{-3}}{2} = \dfrac{1}{2} \pm \mathbf{i}\dfrac{\sqrt{3}}{2}$

  iii. $-\dfrac{1}{2}At^2 + Vt + S = 0$. $x = \dfrac{V \pm \sqrt{V^2 + 2AS}}{A}$

(c) Let $f(x) = x^2 - bx + (b - 1)$. Find $f(1)$. Explain how the Factor Theorem allows you to factor $f(x)$. Then, factor $f(x)$.

$f(1) = 1 - b + (b - 1) = 0$. The Factor Theorem implies that $(x - 1)$ is thus a factor of $f(x)$. So

$$x^2 - bx + (b - 1) = (x - 1)(x - (b - 1)).$$

(d) Show that in $x^2 + bx + c = 0$, the sum of the two roots is $-b$ and the product of the two roots is c. The roots are $x = \frac{-b \pm \sqrt{b^2 - 4c}}{2}$. So,

$$\frac{-b + \sqrt{b^2 - 4c}}{2} + \frac{-b - \sqrt{b^2 - 4c}}{2} = \frac{-2b}{2} = -b,$$

and

$$\left(\frac{-b + \sqrt{b^2 - 4c}}{2}\right)\left(\frac{-b - \sqrt{b^2 - 4c}}{2}\right) = \frac{(-b + \sqrt{b^2 - 4c})(-b - \sqrt{b^2 - 4c})}{4}$$

$$= \frac{(-b)^2 - (b^2 - 4c)}{4} = \frac{4c}{4} = c.$$

(e) Solve $z^2 - iz + 2 = 0$. Using the Quadratic Formula, we get

$$z = \frac{i \pm \sqrt{-1 - 4(2)}}{2} = \frac{i \pm \sqrt{-9}}{2} = \frac{i \pm 3i}{2} = 2i, -i.$$

(f) Solve $x^2 + 3x = -5$. First, we set $x^2 + 3x + 5 = 0$ and use the Quadratic Formula.

$$x = \frac{-3 \pm \sqrt{9 - 4(5)}}{2} = \frac{-3 \pm \sqrt{-11}}{2} = \frac{-3 \pm i\sqrt{11}}{2}.$$

(g) Derive the Quadratic Formula. [Hint: Complete the Square.]

$$ax^2 + bx + c = 0 \qquad \text{Given } (a \neq 0)$$

$$x^2 + \frac{b}{a}x = -\frac{c}{a} \qquad \text{Divide by } a \neq 0 \text{ and rearrange terms}$$

$$x^2 + \frac{b}{a}x + \frac{b^2}{4a^2} = -\frac{c}{a} + \frac{b^2}{4a^2} \qquad \text{Complete the square}$$

$$\left(x + \frac{b}{2a}\right)^2 = \frac{b^2 - 4ac}{4a^2} \qquad \text{Factor, obtain common denominator}$$

$$\left(x + \frac{b}{2a}\right) = \pm\frac{\sqrt{b^2 - 4ac}}{2a} \qquad \text{Take square root of each side}$$

$$x = -\frac{b}{2a} \pm \frac{\sqrt{b^2 - 4ac}}{2a} \qquad \text{Rearrange terms}$$

and thus $x = \dfrac{-b \pm \sqrt{b^2 - 4ac}}{2a}$.

c. Solve polynomial inequalities

1. How do you solve linear inequalities in one variable?

(For more information on linear inequalities with two variables and their graphs, see section **2.3.c**.)

When solving a linear inequality in one variable, one should be able to isolate the variable on one side, and a number on the other, by using standard properties of algebra. See the example in section **2.1.e** above.

2. How do you solve quadratic inequalities in one variable?

Let's compare two examples and then talk about general methods. First, consider $x^2 + 6 > -5x$. By adding $5x$ to both sides, we get $x^2 + 5x + 6 > 0$, or $(x+2)(x+3) > 0$. Now we look at this inequality as saying that a product of two numbers is greater than zero. So either both of these numbers are positive, or both are negative. A quick table will tell us the values of x for which either of these situations holds. Note that the factor $(x+2)$ changes sign at -2, while $(x+3)$ changes sign at -3.

Factor	$x < -3$	$-3 < x < -2$	$-2 < x$
$x + 2$	neg	neg	pos
$x + 3$	neg	pos	pos
$(x+2)(x+3)$	pos	neg	pos

So the solution is $x < -3$ or $x > -2$.

As a second example, consider $x^2 + 6 \le -2x$. This can be transformed to $x^2 + 2x + 6 \le 0$. The left-hand side cannot be factored here. So we need to complete the square instead to get more information. Rewriting, we see

$$x^2 + 2x + 6 \le 0 \implies x^2 + 2x + 1 + 5 \le 0 \implies (x+1)^2 + 5 \le 0,$$

which can be rewritten as $(x+1)^2 \le -5$. Since it is a square of a real number, $(x+1)^2 \ge 0$. So the given inequality has no solutions. (Note that if we had reversed the original inequality to $\ge$, then any value of x would be a solution.)

There are a variety of methods, but I usually try to move all terms to one side of the inequality through addition/subtraction, and then try to factor that side first. If it factors, then you can consider the individual factors and look at the signs of each to determine the answer. If it doesn't factor, then try completing the square to determine more information.

3. How do you solve other polynomial inequalities in one variable?

The previous two methods, factoring and completing the square, can be generalized to some extent. Certainly making a chart of the signs of various factors can be used to determine the sign of their product (or quotient). Completing the square can be used for some polynomials with even highest powers, but that is usually only in very specific instances. See the Sample Problems for higher order polynomial inequalities.

4. Sample Problems

Solve the following inequalities.

(a) $3x + 5 > x - 7$

(b) $4x + 5 \ge x^2 - 7$

(c) $x^2 + 6x > -4$

(d) $(x - a)(x - b) \ge 0$, where $a > b$.

(e) $(3x + 5)(x - 7)(x + 1) < 0$

(f) $x^3 < 1$

(g) $x^4 < 1$

(h) $x^4 - 2x^2 > -2.$

5. Answers to Sample Problems

Solve the following inequalities.

(a) $3x + 5 > x - 7.$ $x > -6$

(b) $4x + 5 \geq x^2 - 7.$ $-2 \leq x \leq 6$

(c) $x^2 + 6x > -4.$ $x > -3 + \sqrt{5}$ or $x < -3 - \sqrt{5}$

   Adding 9 to both sides will complete the square: $(x + 3)^2 > 5$, so $x + 3 > \sqrt{5}$ or $x + 3 < -\sqrt{5}$. The answer follows from these.

(d) $(x - a)(x - b) \geq 0$, where $a > b.$ $x < b$ or $x > a.$

(e) $(3x + 5)(x - 7)(x + 1) < 0.$ $x < -\frac{5}{3}$ or $-1 < x < 7.$

(f) $x^3 < 1.$ $x < 1.$ If you factor $x^3 - 1$, the quadratic factor $x^2 + x + 1$ is always positive. The other factor $x - 1$ determines the sign.

(g) $x^4 < 1.$ $-1 < x < 1.$ If you factor $x^4 - 1$, there is a quadratic factor $x^2 + 1$ which is always positive. The other factors, $x + 1$ and $x - 1$, determine the sign.

(h) $x^4 - 2x^2 > -2.$ True for all real x. To see this, add 1 to both sides to complete the square on the left: $(x^2 - 1)^2 > -1$. Since the left-hand side is a perfect square, it will always be at least zero, and so certainly it will always be greater than -1. The inequality holds for all x.

2.3 Functions

a. Analyze general properties of functions (i.e., domain and range, one-to-one, onto, inverses, composition, and differences between relations and functions) and apply arithmetic operations on functions

1. What is a relation?

   A relation from a set A to a set B is a set of ordered pairs (x, y), where $x \in A$ and $y \in B$.

2. What is a function? What are domain and range?

   A function f from A to B is a relation from A to B that satisfies the following: for every element $x \in A$, there is a unique element $y \in B$ with the property that $(x, y) \in f$. [We say that $y = f(x)$.] In other words, for all $x \in A$, $f(x)$ exists and is unique (meaning there is only one choice for $f(x)$).

   The set A is called the *domain* of f. The set B is called a *codomain* of f. It is not the same thing as the *range* of f. The range of f is $\{f(x) : x \in A\} \subseteq B$.

   Example: $f : \mathbb{R} \to \mathbb{R}$ given by $f(x) = x^2$. The domain of f is $\mathbb{R}$, but the range of f is $[0, \infty)$, the set of non-negative real numbers.

3. What is a one-to-one function?

   A function $f : A \to B$ is one-to-one if, for all $b \in B$, there is at most one $x \in A$ satisfying $f(x) = b$.

   (a) "Blob" Picture: If f is one-to-one, then each element in the domain maps to a unique element in the range.

   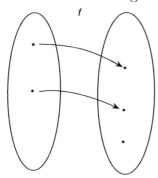

   one-to-one, but not onto

   (b) Graphs and horizontal lines: If f is one-to-one, then each horizontal line intersects the graph at most once. (Ex: $f(x) = \sqrt{x}$.)

   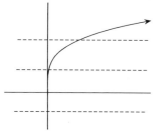

4. What is an onto function?

A function $f : A \to B$ is onto if, for all $b \in B$, there is at least one $x \in A$ satisfying $f(x) = b$.

(a) "Blob" Picture: If f is onto, then each element in the codomain has at least one element mapping to it.

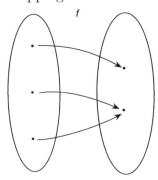

onto, but not one-to-one

(b) Graphs and horizontal lines: If f is onto, then each horizontal line intersects the graph at least once. (Ex: $f(x) = x^3 - x$.)

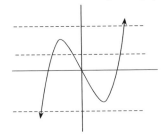

5. How do you make new functions from old functions? How do you apply arithmetic operations on functions?

There are many ways to build new functions from old ones, including the usual arithmetic operations of addition, subtraction, multiplication, and division. These methods include:

(a) shifts (translations)

To shift the graph of $y = f(x)$ up [resp. down] by k units, you _____ [resp. _____] k to the _____ of the function f. The new graph is $y = $ _____[resp. _____].

ANS: add, [subtract], output (or y-value), $f(x) + k$, $[f(x) - k]$.

To shift the graph of $y = f(x)$ right [resp. left] by k units, you _____ [resp. _____] k to the _____ of the function f. The new graph is $y = $ _____[resp. _____].

ANS: subtract, [add], input (or x-value), $f(x - k)$, $[f(x + k)]$.

(b) stretches and smushes (dilations & compressions)

To stretch the graph of $y = f(x)$ vertically by a factor of d units, you _____ the _____ of the function f by d. The new graph is $y = $ _____.

ANS: multiply, output, $df(x)$.

To stretch the graph of $y = f(x)$ horizontally by a factor of d units, you _____ the _____ of the function f by d. The new graph is $y = $ _____.

ANS: divide, input, $f(\frac{x}{d})$.

(c) reflections

To reflect the graph of $y = f(x)$ over the x-axis, you _____ the _____ of the function f by -1. The new graph is $y = $ _____.

ANS: multiply, output, $-f(x)$.

To reflect the graph of $y = f(x)$ over the y-axis, you _____ the _____ of the function f by -1. The new graph is $y = $ _____.

ANS: multiply (or divide!), input, $f(-x)$.

(d) sum, difference, product, quotient

You can add functions f and g to get a new function: $f + g$. The new function is defined by:

$$(f + g)(x) = f(x) + g(x).$$

The other operations are similar, except that there is one restriction when you divide two functions. What is it?

ANS: You are not allowed to divide by zero. If $g(a) = 0$, then a cannot be in the domain of $(f/g)(x) = \frac{f(x)}{g(x)}$.

(e) composition

In addition to addition, subtraction, multiplication, and division, you can compose two functions to obtain a new one. That is, if $f : A \to B$ and $g : B \to C$, then you can compose them to get a new function $h : A \to C$ defined by $h(x) = g(f(x))$. We say $h = g \circ f$.

Example: $f(x) = x^2$ and $g(x) = x + 3$. Then $(g \circ f)(x) = x^2 + 3$ and $(f \circ g)(x) = (x + 3)^2 = x^2 + 6x + 9$. Notice that $f \circ g$ can be different from $g \circ f$.

(f) inverse functions

Also, if a function $f : A \to \text{range}(f)$ is one-to-one, then you can define a new function $f^{-1} : \text{range}(f) \to A$ according to:

$$f^{-1}(b) = x \quad \Longleftrightarrow \quad f(x) = b.$$

The roles of domain and range are swapped.

Example: $f(x) = \dfrac{3x - 5}{7}$. Find f^{-1}.

ANS: The usual algorithm involves switching x and y and then solving for y. That is, instead of $y = \frac{3x-5}{7}$, we start with $x = \frac{3y-5}{7}$, which means $7x = 3y - 5$, or $y = \frac{7x+5}{3}$. So $f^{-1}(x) = \dfrac{7x + 5}{3}$.

The graph of f^{-1} can be obtained from the graph of f by reflecting over the line $y = x$ (which essentially switches y and x, thus swapping the domain and the range).

(g) identity function ($f(x) = x$)

The identity function is a boring function in one sense, but it plays a necessary role both in inverse functions and in function composition. How so?

ANS: The composition of a function and its inverse should be the identity function (because the inverse function "undoes" whatever the original function does). Also, the composition of any function g with the identity function is equal to the function g. (The identity function is "inert" under composition.)

6. Sample Problems

(a) If $f(x) = 2x^2 - 8$ and if $g(x) = \sqrt{x}$, then what is the domain of $g(f(x))$?

(b) Let $f = \{(1,1), (2,3), (2,4), (3,1)\}$ and let $g = \{(4,3), (3,3), (2,1), (1,4)\}$

    i. Which set is a function?

    ii. What is the domain of that function? ... range ...?

    iii. Is that function one-to-one? Explain.

    iv. Is that function onto the set $\{1, 3, 4\}$? Explain.

(c) Fill in the table below. If there is not enough information, put a question mark.

x	1	2	3	4	5
$f(x)$	5	4	3	2	1
$g(x)$	3	5	2	1	4
$(f+g)(x)$					
$(g/f)(x)$					
$(g \circ f)(x)$					
$(f \circ g)(x)$					
$g^{-1}(x)$					

(d) If $f(x) = 3x - 5$, then find $f(f(2))$ and $f^{-1}(2)$.

(e) Sketch the graph of $y = f(x) = |x|$ on the domain $[-2, 2]$. Then sketch the following graphs, labeling the vertex and the endpoints.

    i. $y = f(x) - 3$

    ii. $y = f(x - 3)$

    iii. $y = 3f(x)$

    iv. $y = f(3x)$

    v. $y = -f(x)$

    vi. $y = f(-x)$

(f) Find formulas for the following (separate) transformations of $f(x) = x^3 - x$.

    i. Shift f to the right 4 units and then up 2 units.

    ii. Stretch f horizontally by a factor of 5 and then reflect in the y-axis.

iii. Shift f to the left 3 units, then reflect in the x-axis, and then compress vertically by a factor of 2.

(g) Give an example of functions f and g where $f \neq g$, neither function is the identity, but $f \circ g = g \circ f$.

(h) Find $f^{-1}(x)$ if $f(x) = \frac{5x-2}{3}$. Verify that $f(f^{-1}(x)) = x$ and that $f^{-1}(f(x)) = x$.

7. Answers to Sample Problems

(a) If $f(x) = 2x^2 - 8$ and if $g(x) = \sqrt{x}$, then what is the domain of $g(f(x))$? First, note that $g(f(x)) = \sqrt{2x^2 - 8}$. Its domain is $(-\infty, -2] \cup [2, \infty)$.

(b) Let $f = \{(1,1), (2,3), (2,4), (3,1)\}$ and let $g = \{(4,3), (3,3), (2,1), (1,4)\}$

    i. Which set is a function? g. f is not a function.

    ii. What is the domain of that function? $\{4,3,2,1\}$ range? $\{1,3,4\}$.

    iii. Is that function one-to-one? Explain. NO. $g(4) = g(3) = 3$. Two elements of the domain map to the same element of the range, which means that g is not one-to-one.

    iv. Is that function onto the set $\{1,3,4\}$? Explain. YES. Since g maps to 1, 3, and 4, we say that g is onto the set $\{1,3,4\}$.

(c) Fill in the table below. If there is not enough information, put a question mark.

x	1	2	3	4	5
$f(x)$	5	4	3	2	1
$g(x)$	3	5	2	1	4
$(f+g)(x)$	8	9	5	3	5
$(g/f)(x)$	3/5	5/4	2/3	1/2	4
$(g \circ f)(x)$	4	1	2	5	3
$(f \circ g)(x)$	3	1	4	5	2
$g^{-1}(x)$	4	3	1	5	2

(d) If $f(x) = 3x - 5$, then find $f(f(2))$ and $f^{-1}(2)$. Since $f(2) = 1$, $f(f(2)) = f(1) = -2$. We can find the inverse function directly or use the definition:

$$y = f^{-1}(2) \Leftrightarrow f(y) = 2.$$

So we need to solve $2 = f(y) = 3y - 5$, or $y = f^{-1}(2) = \frac{7}{3}$.

(e) Sketch the graph of $y = f(x) = |x|$ on the domain $[-2,2]$. Then sketch the following graphs, labeling the vertex and the endpoints. Labels have been left off of the answers, but for the original graph, the vertex is at $(0,0)$, and the endpoints are $(-2,2)$ and $(2,2)$.

    i. $y = f(x) - 3 = |x| - 3$, vertex: $(0,-3)$, endpts: $(-2,-1)$ and $(2,-1)$

    ii. $y = f(x-3) = |x-3|$, vertex: $(3,0)$, endpts: $(1,2)$ and $(5,2)$

    iii. $y = 3f(x) = 3|x|$, vertex: $(0,0)$, endpts: $(-2,6)$ and $(2,6)$

    iv. $y = f(3x) = |3x|$, vertex: $(0,0)$, endpts: $\left(-\frac{2}{3}, 2\right)$ and $\left(\frac{2}{3}, 2\right)$

v. $y = -f(x) = -|x|$, vertex: $(0,0)$, endpts: $(-2, -2)$ and $(2, -2)$

vi. $y = f(-x) = |-x| = |x|$ (same as original graph)

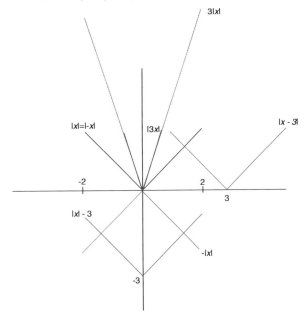

(f) Find formulas for the following (separate) transformations of $f(x) = x^3 - x$.

  i. Shift f to the right 4 units and then up 2 units. $(x-4)^3 - (x-4) + 2$

  ii. Stretch f horizontally by a factor of 5 and then reflect in the y-axis. $-(\frac{x}{5})^3 + \frac{x}{5}$

  iii. Shift f to the left 3 units, then reflect in the x-axis, and then compress vertically by a factor of 2. $\frac{1}{2}[(-x+3)^3 - (-x+3)]$

(g) Give an example of functions f and g where $f \neq g$, neither function is the identity, but $f \circ g = g \circ f$. There are many answers. For example, $f(x) = x + 3$ and $g(x) = x - 5$. Also, $f(x) = px$ and $g(x) = qx$, where p and q are any real numbers with $p \neq q$.

(h) Find $f^{-1}(x)$ if $f(x) = \frac{5x-2}{3}$. Verify that $f(f^{-1}(x)) = x$ and that $f^{-1}(f(x)) = x$.

$$f^{-1}(x) = \frac{3x + 2}{5}.$$

$$f(f^{-1}(x)) = f\left(\frac{3x + 2}{5}\right)$$

$$= \frac{5\left(\frac{3x+2}{5}\right) - 2}{3} = \frac{3x + 2 - 2}{3} = x.$$

$$f^{-1}(f(x)) = f^{-1}\left(\frac{5x - 2}{3}\right)$$

$$= \frac{3\left(\frac{5x-2}{3}\right) + 2}{5} = \frac{5x - 2 + 2}{5} = x.$$

b. Analyze properties of linear functions (e.g., slope, intercepts) using a variety of representations

1. What is a linear equation?

Let's begin with what is called the Standard Form of a linear equation: $Ax + By = C$, where A, B, and C are real numbers (and A and B are not both equal to zero). Any linear equation can be put into this form, and any equation in this form is a linear equation.

Another common form is as a linear *function*, which is often written $y = mx + b$. Any linear function can be put into Standard Form, but there are some linear equations that are not linear functions (e.g., if $B = 0$ in the Standard Form).

2. What does the graph of a linear equation look like?

   One nice feature of the Standard Form of a linear equation is that the graph of its solution set is a straight line on the xy-plane. Conversely, any line on the xy-plane is the solution set to some linear equation.

   Linear function graphs are also straight lines, but not every straight line is the graph of a linear function (e.g., vertical lines are not graphs of functions).

3. What are the important features of a linear equation, and how do they relate to its graph?

   Probably the most important feature mathematically is the ratio of changes in y to changes in x, called the *slope* of the line. It shows up on the graph as the ratio of the "rise" to the "run" of the line. In Standard Form, the slope is $-\frac{A}{B}$, if $B \neq 0$. When $B = 0$, then the slope is not defined, and the line is vertical. See the examples below.

   Also, most lines intersect the y-axis at a unique point called the y-intercept. Since it is the point where $x = 0$, it can be found by setting $x = 0$ in the Standard Form and then solving for y. Hence, $By = C$, or $y = \frac{C}{B}$ (assuming $B \neq 0$). When $B = 0$ in the Standard Form equation, then the corresponding line is vertical, and it does not have a y-intercept.

   Instead, a vertical line has a constant x-coordinate. Since $B = 0$ in the Standard Form for vertical lines, we can solve for x to find the equation of the line. Hence, $Ax = C$, or $x = \frac{C}{A}$. We know that A is not zero, because we said earlier that A and B cannot both be zero in the Standard Form.

   Incidentally, x-intercepts can also be looked at. Since it is the point where $y = 0$, it can be found by setting $y = 0$ in the Standard Form and then solving for x. Hence, $Ax = C$, or $x = \frac{C}{A}$ (assuming $A \neq 0$). If $A = 0$, then the corresponding line is horizontal, its slope is zero, and its equation is $y = \frac{C}{B}$.

4. What are some different forms of a linear equation?

   First, we will find a formula for the slope. The slope m of the line passing through (x_1, y_1) and (x_2, y_2) is $m = \dfrac{y_2 - y_1}{x_2 - x_1}$ (assuming $x_1 \neq x_2$). If $x_1 = x_2$, then the line is vertical, and its slope is not defined.

   Slope-Intercept Form: If a line has slope m and y-intercept b, then its equation is $y = mx + b$.

   Point-Slope Form: If a line has slope m and passes through (h, k), then its equation is $y - k = m(x - h)$.

5. What are some examples of linear equations and their graphs?

(a) $x = 3$; $y = 4$. Here, we have one vertical and one horizontal line. To graph them, you can plot a few points. For instance, for the equation $x = 3$, there are several points that satisfy that equation: $(3, 0)$, $(3, 1)$, and $(3, 3)$, to name just a few. Similarly, any point with a y-coordinate of 4 will satisfy the equation $y = 4$. The two graphs are given below.

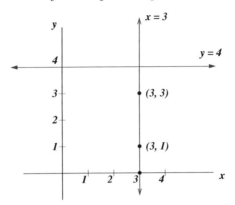

(b) $x + y = 2$; $x - 2y = 2$. Here we have one line with negative slope $m = -1$ (down to the right) and one line with positive slope $m = \frac{1}{2}$ (up to the right). To graph these lines, one can either choose an x-value and plug it in to the equation to determine its corresponding y-value, or you can put the line into Slope-Intercept Form algebraically. Then, plotting its y-intercept and its slope leads to the line. So, $x + y = 2$ becomes $y = -x + 2$, which has slope -1 and y-intercept 2. Similarly, $x - 2y = 2$ becomes $y = \frac{1}{2}x - 1$, which has slope $\frac{1}{2}$ and y-intercept -1.

The two graphs are given below.

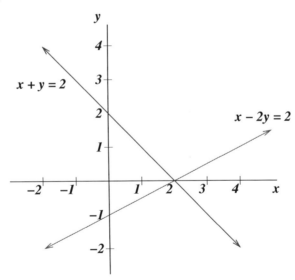

6. What are the slope criteria for parallel lines? ... for perpendicular lines?

Two distinct lines are parallel if 1) they are both vertical, or 2) they have the same slope. (Recall that slope is not defined for vertical lines.) Two lines are perpendicular if 1) one is vertical and one is horizontal, or 2) the product of their slopes is -1. Another way to say this is that their slopes are negative reciprocals of each other. (For a proof of these facts (and more), see my book *Common Core State Standards for High School Math: Geometry - What Every Math Teacher Should Know*, Createspace, 2012.)

7. Sample Problems

   (a) Graph the following: $3x + 2y = 5$, $x = -3$, and $x - y = 0$. Put each equation in Slope-Intercept Form, if possible.

   (b) Find a Point-Slope form of the line that passes through $(2, -4)$ and is parallel to $4x - 3y = 2$.

   (c) Find a line that is perpendicular to the line through $(1, -3)$ and $(4, 2)$, but passes through the point $(1, 5)$.

   (d) There is a linear equation relating a temperature on the Fahrenheit scale to its value on the Celsius scale. You know that zero degrees Celsius corresponds to 32 degrees Fahrenheit, and that 100 degrees Celsius corresponds to 212 degrees Fahrenheit. Sketch a graph of temperature Fahrenheit versus temperature Celsius. What is the slope of the graph? What is the linear formula giving Fahrenheit temperature as a function of Celsius temperature?

8. Answers to Sample Problems

   (a) Graph the following: $3x + 2y = 5$, $x = -3$, and $x - y = 0$. Put each equation in Slope-Intercept Form, if possible.

   The Slope-Intercept Form is not possible for $x = -3$ because this line is vertical and therefore does not have a defined slope. However, using algebra, $3x + 2y = 5$ can be written as $y = -\frac{3}{2}x + \frac{5}{2}$. Also, $x - y = 0$ can be written as $y = x$. The graphs are below.

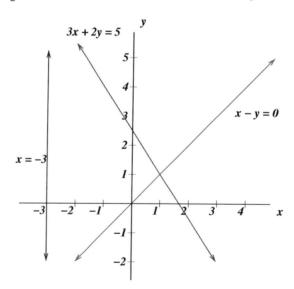

   (b) Find a Point-Slope form of the line that passes through $(2, -4)$ and is parallel to $4x - 3y = 2$. The slope of $4x - 3y = 2$ can be found by putting the equation into Slope-Intercept

Form (i.e., $y = \frac{4}{3}x - \frac{2}{3}$), or by knowing that in Standard Form, the slope is $-\frac{A}{B}$. Either route leads to a slope of $\frac{4}{3}$. So, our desired line is

$$y + 4 = \frac{4}{3}(x - 2).$$

(c) Find a line that is perpendicular to the line through $(1, -3)$ and $(4, 2)$, but passes through the point $(1, 5)$.

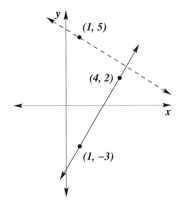

The slope through $(1, -3)$ and $(4, 2)$ is $\frac{2+3}{4-1} = \frac{5}{3}$. Since we want a line perpendicular to this one, the slope we want is $-\frac{3}{5}$. So we need a line with slope $-\frac{3}{5}$ and passing through the point $(1, 5)$. Using the Point-Slope form of the line, we get

$$y - 5 = -\frac{3}{5}(x - 1).$$

(d) There is a linear equation relating a temperature on the Fahrenheit scale to its value on the Celsius scale. You know that zero degrees Celsius corresponds to 32 degrees Fahrenheit, and that 100 degrees Celsius corresponds to 212 degrees Fahrenheit. Sketch a graph of temperature Fahrenheit versus temperature Celsius. What is the slope of the graph? What is the linear formula giving Fahrenheit temperature as a function of Celsius temperature?

We will graph Fahrenheit temperature (F) as a function of Celsius temperature (C). That means that F goes on the y-axis and C on the x-axis. The two known points we have are $(0, 32)$ and $(100, 212)$. See the graph below.

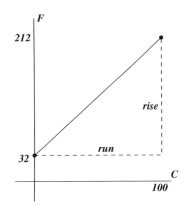

So the slope is the rise divided by the run, or $\dfrac{212-32}{100-0} = \dfrac{180}{100} = \dfrac{9}{5}$. Thus the formula is

$$F - 32 = \frac{9}{5}(C - 0) \quad \text{or} \quad F = \frac{9}{5}C + 32.$$

c. Demonstrate knowledge of why graphs of linear inequalities are half planes and be able to apply this fact

1. Why is the graph of a linear inequality a half plane?

   If you can solve the inequality for y, then it is clear that you are looking for values of y either above $(y > f(x))$ or below $(y < f(x))$ the line. If y doesn't appear in the equation, then the line must be vertical, and the inequality tells you if you are looking for points to the right $(x > a)$ or to the left $(x < a)$ of this line. In the following examples, the boundary lines have been labeled. Dotted boundary lines are not part of the solution set.

   Examples: $y \leq 5, \quad x > -2, \quad x + 2y \geq 3$

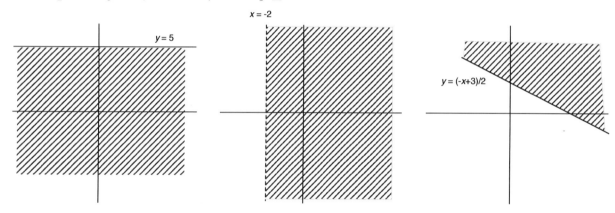

2. How do you apply linear inequalities?

   Linear programming can be used to solve optimization problems in many different fields. Usually, you are asked to maximize some quantity with respect to various linear constraints.

   Simple(x) Example: Say you have 20 days to knit hats and scarves for a friend's store. It takes you 1.5 days to knit a hat and only 1 day to knit a scarf. You plan to charge \$20 per hat and \$15 per scarf, but your friend says that she wants no more than 16 items from you. How many hats and how many scarves should you knit in order to maximize your revenue?

   ANS: Let x be the number of hats knitted and y the number of scarves knitted. So $x \geq 0$ and $y \geq 0$. Also, $x + y \leq 16$ because your friend only wants 16 items at most. The number of days it takes to knit hats is $1.5x$, while the number of days it takes to knit scarves is y. So $1.5x + y \leq 20$ since there are only 20 days to knit. If we graph all of these inequalities, we obtain a region of all the possible numbers of scarves and hats you could knit. The revenue function is $20x + 15y$, which we would like to maximize on the given region. According to the simplex method, since the revenue condition is linear, we need only check the corners of our region, which occur at any intersection point of two linear conditions.

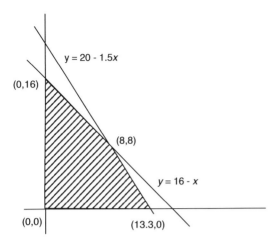

Checking, we get:

- no scarves and no hats yields 0 dollars of revenue

- 16 scarves and no hats yields $(16)(15) = 240$ dollars of revenue

- 8 scarves and 8 hats yields $8(15) + 8(20) = 280$ dollars of revenue

- 13 hats and no scarves yields $13(20) = 260$ dollars of revenue

So, to maximize revenue, you should knit eight scarves and eight hats.

3. Sample Problems

   (a) Sketch the solution to $y \leq 2x - 5$.

   (b) Sketch the solution to $2x + 3y > 6$.

   (c) Sketch all the complex numbers $a + bi$ with $a \leq 2b$.

   (d) Suppose that a company makes two kinds of puzzles: easy and hard. The company has 10 weeks to make puzzles before putting the products on the market. They can make 60 easy puzzles per week and 40 hard puzzles per week. They make \$12 profit on each easy puzzle and \$15 profit on each hard puzzle. Assuming that they can only put 500 puzzles on the market, how many of each should they make?

4. Answers to Sample Problems

   (a) Sketch the solution to $y \leq 2x - 5$.

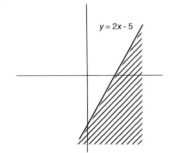

(b) Sketch the solution to $2x + 3y > 6$.

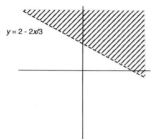

$y = 2 - 2x/3$

(c) Sketch all the complex numbers $a + bi$ with $a \le 2b$.

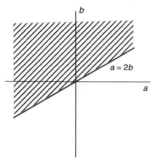

b

$a = 2b$

a

(d) Suppose that a company makes two kinds of puzzles: easy and hard. The company has 10 weeks to make puzzles before putting the products on the market. They can make 60 easy puzzles per week and 40 hard puzzles per week. They make \$12 profit on each easy puzzle and \$15 profit on each hard puzzle. Assuming that they can only put 500 puzzles on the market, how many of each should they make? 300 easy, 200 hard.

The corners of the region of interest are $(0,0)$, $(0,400)$, $(500,0)$, and $(300,200)$, where x is the number of easy puzzles made and y is the number of hard puzzles made. Checking each one, we obtain the maximum revenue at $(300,200)$.

d. Analyze properties of polynomial, rational, radical, and absolute value functions in a variety of ways (e.g., graphing, solving problems)

1. Continuity and holes

Polynomials and absolute value functions are continuous on the entire domain of real numbers. Rational functions are continuous everywhere except when the denominator is zero. Radical functions are continuous on their domains, but are not always defined for all reals.

Examples include: $3x^3 - x$, $|x - 4|$, $\dfrac{x+3}{x^2-4}$ (discontinuities at $x = \pm 2$), and $\sqrt{x-2}$ (not defined for $x < 2$).

2. Intercepts, horizontal and vertical

Every function has exactly one vertical intercept, provided that $x = 0$ is in its domain. Functions can have several horizontal intercepts, which can be found by setting the value of the function to zero and solving for x. For example, $x^3 - 2x + 1$ has one vertical intercept at $y = 1$, and three horizontal intercepts: $\dfrac{-1 \pm \sqrt{5}}{2}$ and 1.

3. Asymptotes, horizontal and vertical

Polynomials, radicals, and absolute value functions have no asymptotes. Rational functions have horizontal asymptotes exactly when the degree of the numerator is less than or equal to the degree of the denominator. Rational functions can have vertical asymptotes or holes at the points where the denominator is zero. How can you tell which is which? (See example.)

Example: $f(x) = \dfrac{x^2 + 4x + 4}{x^2 - 4}$ versus $g(x) = \dfrac{x^2 + 2x + 1}{x^2 - 4}$

$f(x)$ can be factored and reduced to $\dfrac{x+2}{x-2}$, provided that $x \neq -2$. This means that there is a hole in the graph of f at the point $\left(-2, \frac{-2+2}{-2-2}\right) = (-2, 0)$. The function $g(x)$ cannot be reduced, which means that the $(x+2)$ factor cannot be canceled. Thus $g(x)$ has a vertical asymptote at $x = -2$.

4. Sample Problems

   (a) Solve for x: $\sqrt{x} + \sqrt{x+3} = 3$.

   (b) Find the range of $f(x) = |2x - 5| + 3$ and sketch the graph of $y = f(x)$.

   (c) Say that $y = f(x)$ is a cubic polynomial and that $f(3) = f(1) = f(-2) = 0$. Also, say that $f(0) = 12$. Find the formula for f.

   (d) What is the [subtle] difference between $f(x) = x + 1$ and $g(x) = \dfrac{x^2 - 1}{x - 1}$? How does this show up on their graphs?

   (e) Explain why the domain of $\sqrt{x}$ is $[0, \infty)$ but the domain of $\sqrt[3]{x}$ is all real numbers.

   (f) Sketch a graph of $y = \dfrac{x^2 - 1}{x^2 - 4}$, labeling all intercepts and asymptotes.

   (g) Sketch a graph of $y = \dfrac{1}{x^2 + 1}$, labeling all intercepts and asymptotes.

   (h) Sketch $y = \sqrt{x}$. Then sketch its inverse graph and find the formula. What is the domain of f^{-1} in this case?

   (i) Explain why $f(x) = x^2$ is not invertible on its domain of all real numbers, but that it is invertible on the restricted domain $[0, \infty)$.

5. Answers to Sample Problems

   (a) Solve for x: $\sqrt{x} + \sqrt{x+3} = 3$. $x = 1$

   (b) Find the range of $f(x) = |2x - 5| + 3$ and sketch the graph of $y = f(x)$. The range is $[3, \infty)$.

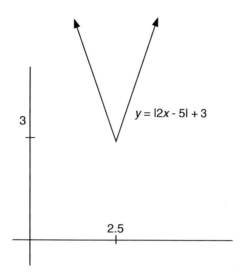

$y = |2x - 5| + 3$

3

2.5

(c) Say that $y = f(x)$ is a cubic polynomial and that $f(3) = f(1) = f(-2) = 0$. Also, say that $f(0) = 12$. Find the formula for f. $f(x) = 2(x-3)(x-1)(x+2) = 2x^3 - 4x^2 - 10x + 12$

(d) What is the [subtle] difference between $f(x) = x + 1$ and $g(x) = \dfrac{x^2 - 1}{x - 1}$? How does this show up on their graphs?

The only difference is that 1 is in the domain of f but it is not in the domain of g. Other than that, the two functions are identical. This means that the graph of $y = g(x)$ is the line $x + 1$ except that it has a hole at the point $(1, 2)$.

(e) Explain why the domain of $\sqrt{x}$ is $[0, \infty)$ but the domain of $\sqrt[3]{x}$ is all real numbers. The square root of a negative number is not real, whereas the cube root of a negative number is negative. For example, since $(-2)^3 = -8$, $\sqrt[3]{-8} = -2$.

(f) Sketch a graph of $y = \dfrac{x^2 - 1}{x^2 - 4}$, labeling all intercepts and asymptotes.

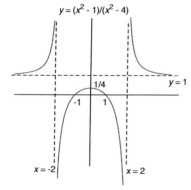

$y = (x^2 - 1)/(x^2 - 4)$

1/4

$y = 1$

-1   1

$x = -2$ $x = 2$

(g) Sketch a graph of $y = \dfrac{1}{x^2 + 1}$, labeling all intercepts and asymptotes.

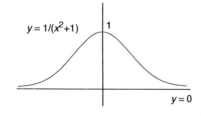

$y = 1/(x^2 + 1)$

1

$y = 0$

(h) Sketch $y = \sqrt{x}$. Then sketch its inverse graph and find the formula. What is the domain of f^{-1} in this case? The domain of the inverse function is $[0, \infty)$.

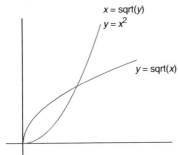

(i) Explain why $f(x) = x^2$ is not invertible on its domain of all real numbers, but that it is invertible on the restricted domain $[0, \infty)$. The function $f(x) = x^2$ is not one-to-one on its domain, $((-2)^2 = 2^2 = 4$, for instance), but it *is* one-to-one on its restricted domain. That means that f is invertible if we only consider non-negative values of x.

e. Analyze properties of exponential and logarithmic functions in a variety of ways (e.g., graphing, solving problems)

*** *For a quick review of logarithms, see the Miscellaneous Topics at the end of this book.*

1. How are exponential and logarithmic functions related?

   The exponential and logarithmic functions are inverse functions of each other. So,

   - $y = e^x \Leftrightarrow x = \ln y$,
   - $y = 10^x \Leftrightarrow x = \log y$, and in general,
   - $y = b^x \Leftrightarrow x = \log_b y$.

2. Continuity

   The basic exponential functions are continuous on the entire domain of real numbers.

   The basic logarithmic functions are continuous on their domains (positive real numbers).

3. Intercepts, horizontal and vertical

   The basic exponential functions have only one intercept, at $(0, 1)$.

   The basic logarithmic functions have only one intercept, at $(1, 0)$.

4. Asymptotes, horizontal and vertical

   Exponential functions have one horizontal asymptote, at $y = 0$. As an example, $\lim\limits_{x \to -\infty} 2^x = 0$.

   Logarithmic functions have one vertical asymptote, at $x = 0$. For example, as $x \to 0^+$, $\ln x \to -\infty$.

5. Sample Problems

   (a) Explain the domains and ranges, intercepts, and asymptotes of basic exponential and logarithmic functions in terms of inverse functions.

(b) Simplify, if possible:

    i. $e^{\ln 4}$

    ii. $\ln(e^{3x})$

    iii. $\log 200 + \log 50$

    iv. $\log_3(2) - \log_3(18)$

    v. $\log_b 1$

    vi. $\log_b 0$

    vii. $10^{\log x + \log x^2}$

(c) Solve for x: $3 - \log x = 10$.

(d) Solve for x: $\ln 2^x = \ln 3$.

(e) Suppose that the value of your \$20,000 car depreciates by 10% each year after you bought it. Find a formula for the value of your car V as a function of t, the number of years since you bought it.

(f) Suppose that you have money in a bank account earning 5% interest. Then the amount of money you have after t years is given by $A(t) = P(1.05)^t$. where P is the principal amount invested. Find the doubling time of this account. Leave logarithms in your answer.

(g) Find a formula for an exponential function that passes through the point $(0, 4)$ and the point $(1, 8)$.

(h) Sketch a rough graph of $y = 5 - e^{-x}$. [Hint: Use transformations of a basic graph.] Name a real-world process you could model with a graph of this shape.

6. Answers to Sample Problems

(a) Explain the domains and ranges, intercepts, and asymptotes of basic exponential and logarithmic functions in terms of inverse functions.

Feature	Exponential	Logarithmic
Domain	all reals	$x > 0$
Range	$y > 0$	all reals
Intercepts	$y = 1$	$x = 1$
Asymptotes	$y = 0$	$x = 0$

Notice that switching x and y (reflecting over the line $y = x$) takes the domain of one function to the range of the other and vice versa. Also, the $y = 1$ intercept of a basic exponential function switches with the $x = 1$ intercept of a basic logarithmic function. Similarly, the horizontal asymptote of a basic exponential function switches with the vertical asymptote of a basic logarithmic function.

(b) Simplify, if possible:

    i. $e^{\ln 4} = 4$

    ii. $\ln(e^{3x}) = 3x$

    iii. $\log 200 + \log 50 = \log 10{,}000 = 4$

    iv. $\log_3(2) - \log_3(18) = \log_3 \frac{1}{9} = -2$

    v. $\log_b 1 = 0$

   vi. $\log_b 0$ is not defined.

  vii. $10^{\log x + \log x^2} = 10^{\log x^3} = x^3$

(c) Solve for x: $3 - \log x = 10$. $x = 10^{-7}$

(d) Solve for x: $\ln 2^x = \ln 3$. $2^x = 3$; $x = \log_2 3 = \frac{\ln 3}{\ln 2} = \frac{\log 3}{\log 2}$

(e) Suppose that the value of your \$20,000 car depreciates by 10% each year after you bought it. Find a formula for the value of your car V as a function of t, the number of years since you bought it. $V(t) = 20{,}000(0.9)^t$

(f) Suppose that you have money in a bank account earning 5% interest. Then the amount of money you have after t years is given by $A(t) = P(1.05)^t$. where P is the principal amount invested. Find the doubling time of this account. Leave logarithms in your answer.

If $2P = P(1.05)^t$, then $2 = (1.05)^t$, or $t = \log_{1.05} 2 = \frac{\ln 2}{\ln 1.05} = \frac{\log 2}{\log 1.05}$.

(g) Find a formula for an exponential function that passes through the point $(0, 4)$ and the point $(1, 8)$. $y = 4 \cdot 2^x$

(h) Sketch a rough graph of $y = 5 - e^{-x}$. [Hint: Use transformations of a basic graph.] Name a real-world process you could model with a graph of this shape.

Using transformations: you can start with $y = e^x$, flip it over the y-axis to get $y = e^{-x}$, then flip it over the x-axis to get $y = -e^{-x}$. Finally, shift it up five units.

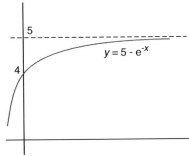

One possible process is heating an object. As the object sits in an oven (at a constant temperature), the object's temperature exponentially approaches the temperature of the oven. There are other valid answers.

f. Model and solve problems using nonlinear functions

There are similarities between this section and **1.1.c** and **2.1.f**. We will include a linear example here just to keep most of the modeling problems in one place.

1. What are some linear and quadratic examples of modeling and solving problems?

We will begin with a linear example to help set the stage. Assume that your cell phone contract costs \$20 a month plus \$0.05 per minute for calls. We'll ignore texting and data. Suppose your bill for last month was \$42.15. We can write an equation to represent this. If we let m represent the number of minutes spent calling, then the total cost of those minutes is $0.05m$, and so the cost of your monthly bill is $20 + 0.05m$. So, our equation representing last month's bill is:

$$20 + 0.05m = 42.15.$$

Suppose that we want the bill to be at most \$40. We can write that as an inequality: $20 + 0.05m \leq 40$.

For solving the equation $20 + 0.05m = 42.15$, we subtract 20 from both sides, giving $0.05m = 22.15$. Next we divide by 0.05 (or multiply by 20), to get $m = 443$. So the total usage that month was 443 minutes.

For a quadratic example, let's turn to economics – to revenue in particular. One simple model says that the price of a product determines the quantity sold. Let's suppose that the quantity sold is $3250 - 25p$, where p is the price of the item in dollars. Now suppose that the total revenue is \$32,725. We can write an equation to represent this. Since the revenue is the total amount of money coming in, it must equal the product of the quantity sold and the price. So, our equation is

$$(3250 - 25p)p = 32{,}725 \quad \text{or} \quad 3250p - 25p^2 = 32{,}725.$$

Suppose that we want a revenue of at least \$100,000. Then we can write that as an inequality: $3250p - 25p^2 \geq 100{,}000$.

To solve this inequality, we add $-3250p + 25p^2$ to both sides. (There are other methods; I find it easier to have a positive leading coefficient on the quadratic term.) This gives

$$0 \geq 25p^2 - 3250p + 100{,}000 \quad \text{or} \quad 0 \geq p^2 - 130p + 4000 = (p - 50)(p - 80).$$

So since $0 \geq (p - 50)(p - 80)$, we need one factor to be positive and one to be negative. This happens in the region between 50 and 80. So the solution would be $50 \leq p \leq 80$. In the terms of the original problem, the revenue will exceed \$100,000 when the price is between \$50 and \$80.

2. What are some rational and exponential examples of modeling and solving problems?

The rational expression $\dfrac{k}{x^2}$ can be used to model the behavior of certain physical quantities, such as the force due to gravity between two bodies that are separated by a distance, x, where k is a nonzero constant. If you wanted to determine the value(s) of x for which this force is equal to $\dfrac{2k}{3}$, you could create the equation $\dfrac{k}{x^2} = \dfrac{2k}{3}$. If you wanted to know the values of x for which the force is greater than $2k$, you would create the inequality $\dfrac{k}{x^2} > 2k$.

To solve the equation $\dfrac{k}{x^2} = \dfrac{2k}{3}$, we can clear denominators by multiplying through by $3x^2$. This gives the new equation $3k = 2kx^2$. Since $k \neq 0$, we can divide by $2k$ to get $x^2 = \dfrac{3}{2}$. So $x = \pm\sqrt{\dfrac{3}{2}}$. Since x represents the distance between two bodies, only the positive answer makes sense. So $x = \sqrt{\dfrac{3}{2}}$.

For an exponential example, you may recall the expression $P(1 + r)^t$ that represents the amount of money in a bank account, where P is the initial deposit, r is the annual interest rate, and t is the number of years that have passed since the initial deposit. The interest is compounded annually. How long does it take for \$5000 to grow to \$7500 in an account bearing 4.5% interest, compounded annually?

To solve this, we first need to set up the correct equation. Here, $P = 5000$, $r = 0.045$, and the entire expression is equal to 7500. That is,

$$5000(1.045)^t = 7500.$$

Next, we divide both sides by 5000, to get $1.045^t = \dfrac{3}{2}$. Taking a logarithm (let's use natural log) of both sides gives

$$\ln(1.045^t) = \ln\frac{3}{2} \quad \text{or} \quad t\ln 1.045 = \ln 1.5.$$

We used a property of logarithms to help simplify. So $t = \dfrac{\ln 1.5}{\ln 1.045} \approx 9.212$. So if the interest is compounded annually, it would take ten years before the bank account rose above \$7500. (Nine years would not be long enough.)

If we wanted to know when the account had more than \$8000 dollars, then we could solve the inequality: $5000(1.045)^t > 8000$.

3. Sample Problems

   (a) The time it takes to drive 60 miles depends on how fast you are driving. Write an equation describing this situation in terms of t, the time the journey takes, and v, the speed at which you are driving. Sketch a graph of t as a function of v.

   (b) Create an equation for P and t, where P is the population of bacteria in a Petri dish at time t. Assume the initial population is 1000 bacteria, and that the population doubles every hour. Is this linear growth or exponential growth? Explain.

   (c) The time, t, that it takes to grade papers depends on n, the number of papers you have to grade. Assuming it takes 7 minutes to prepare the answer key and then 3 minutes to grade each paper, write down an equation relating t and n. Sketch a graph of t as a function of n.

   (d) You may recall that the formula for a Celsius temperature C, is related to its equivalent Fahrenheit temperature F via: $C = \frac{5}{9}(F - 32)$. Manipulate this equation so that the Fahrenheit temperature is isolated. What does the formula tell us now?

   (e) The area, A, of a circle depends on its radius, r: $A = \pi r^2$. Solve this equation for r. What does the formula tell us now?

4. Answers to Sample Problems

   (a) The time it takes to drive 60 miles depends on how fast you are driving. Write an equation describing this situation in terms of t, the time the journey takes, and v, the speed at which you are driving. Sketch a graph of t as a function of v.

There are a few ways to reach this answer. One is to recall that "rate times time equals distance." So $vt = 60$, or $t = \dfrac{60}{v}$. Another way is to think about a few points. How long would the journey take if you drove 60mph? One hour. What if you drove 30mph? Two hours. What if you drove 120mph? Then the journey would only take half an hour. So these also satisfy $t = \dfrac{60}{v}$.

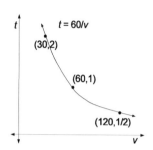

(b) Create an equation for P and t, where P is the population of bacteria in a Petri dish at time t. Assume the initial population is 1000 bacteria, and that the population doubles every hour. Is this linear growth or exponential growth? Explain.

We'll answer the second part first. This set-up is an example of exponential growth. Linear growth would increase by the same *amount* every hour, whereas exponential growth increases by the same *factor* every hour. Let's compare these two models in a table, assuming each model starts with 1000 bacteria and has 2000 bacteria after one hour.

t (in hours)	0	1	2	3
Linear	1000	2000	3000	4000
Exponential	1000	2000	4000	8000

Now let's find a formula for the exponential population, because that is the one we want. First, let's divide each entry by 1000 so we can see what is going on. Then, our population is 1, 2, 4, and 8. Notice that these are powers of 2: 2^0, 2^1, 2^2, and 2^3. In general, we get 2^t. So the population satisfies $P = 1000 \cdot 2^t$. (You could also think of it as a 100% growth rate each hour. Then we would use $r = 1$ in the interest formula, $P = 1000(1 + r)^t$, to get $P = 1000(1 + 1)^t = 1000 \cdot 2^t$.)

(c) The time, t, that it takes to grade papers depends on n, the number of papers you have to grade. Assuming it takes 7 minutes to prepare the answer key and then 3 minutes to grade each paper, write down an equation relating t and n. Sketch a graph of t as a function of n.

$t = 7 + 3n$

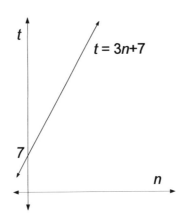

(d) You may recall that the formula for a Celsius temperature C, is related to its equivalent Fahrenheit temperature F via: $C = \frac{5}{9}(F - 32)$. Manipulate this equation so that the Fahrenheit temperature is isolated. What does the formula tell us now?

We would get $F = \frac{9}{5}C + 32$. Now the formula tells us which Fahrenheit temperature corresponds to a given Celsius temperature. In other words, if you know the temperature in degrees Celsius, then this formula is more useful in finding the equivalent Fahrenheit temperature.

(e) The area, A, of a circle depends on its radius, r: $A = \pi r^2$. Solve this equation for r. What does the formula tell us now?

We would get $r = \sqrt{\dfrac{A}{\pi}}$. This tells us the radius of a circle if we know its area. (Since the radius of a circle cannot be negative, we do not use a $\pm$ sign.)

2.4 Linear Algebra

a. Understand and apply the geometric interpretation and basic operations of vectors in two and three dimensions, including their scalar multiples

1. What is a vector?

   A vector is a mathematical object that has a magnitude and a direction. People often think of two-dimensional (2-D) vectors as arrows drawn on the plane, and three-dimensional (3-D) vectors as arrows in space. The starting point of a vector is not important to the definition. Consequently, vectors are often depicted in *standard position* (starting at the origin). The magnitude (or length) of $\vec{v}$ is often denoted $\|\vec{v}\|$.

2. What is a vector space?

   A vector space is a set (made up of elements called vectors) that is closed under an operation called vector addition (which is commutative and associative and has an identity and inverses) and under multiplication by a field of scalars (usually the real numbers) which has nice associative and distributive properties over vector addition. The main examples of vector spaces for us will be $\mathbb{R}^2$ (the Cartesian coordinate plane) and $\mathbb{R}^3$ (three-dimensional space).

3. How do you write vectors?

   There are three common main ways to write vectors:

   (a) as ordered n-tuples: $\langle 1, -2 \rangle$ or $\langle -3, 0, 4 \rangle$, [or sometimes as $(1, -2)$ or $(-3, 0, 4)$]

   (b) in terms of component vectors: $\vec{i} - 2\vec{j}$ or $-3\vec{i} + 4\vec{k}$, or

   (c) as columns: $\begin{bmatrix} 1 \\ -2 \end{bmatrix}$ or $\begin{bmatrix} -3 \\ 0 \\ 4 \end{bmatrix}$.

4. How do you add vectors? How do you multiply vectors by scalars?

   Algebraically, you can add vectors by adding their corresponding components. You can multiply a vector by a scalar by multiplying each of its components by that scalar. For example, if $\vec{v} = \langle 1, 4, -6 \rangle$ and $\vec{w} = \langle -3, 0, -2 \rangle$, then:

   $\vec{v} + \vec{w} = \langle 1 + (-3), 4 + 0, (-6) + (-2) \rangle = \langle -2, 4, -8 \rangle$,

   $2\vec{v} = \langle 2(1), 2(4), 2(-6) \rangle = \langle 2, 8, -12 \rangle$,

   and $\vec{v} - \vec{w} = \langle 1 - (-3), 4 - 0, (-6) - (-2) \rangle = \langle 4, 4, -4 \rangle$.

   Geometrically, you can add vectors by drawing one vector at the head of another. You can also multiply a vector by a scalar by scaling the vector by that amount. For example,

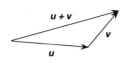
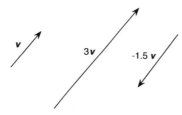

5. How do you "multiply" two vectors?

In general, you cannot multiply vectors, which is one of the ways that they are different from numbers. However, there are two specific products that are useful.

(a) Dot Product (scalar)

The dot product is defined for vectors in any dimension. The dot product of two vectors is always a scalar (and is never a vector). So it's also called the scalar product.

i. Algebraic
If $\vec{v} = \langle v_1, v_2, \ldots, v_n \rangle$ and $\vec{w} = \langle w_1, w_2, \ldots, w_n \rangle$, then

$$\vec{v} \cdot \vec{w} = v_1 w_1 + v_2 w_2 + \ldots + v_n w_n.$$

ii. Geometric
The dot product of two vectors is the product of their lengths times the cosine of the angle between them. That is,

$$\vec{v} \cdot \vec{w} = \|\vec{v}\| \|\vec{w}\| \cos\theta.$$

iii. Why is the dot product important?
The dot product is the easiest way to determine the angle between two vectors. So, it can be used to tell when two vectors are perpendicular. Also, the dot product of a vector with itself gives you the square of the length because $\theta = 0$ in this case. Physicists use the dot product to decompose a vector into its various components. For example, work is the dot product of the force vector with the displacement vector. Force that is perpendicular to the direction of motion ($\theta = 90°$) does not do any work.

(b) Cross Product (vector)

The cross product is only defined for three-dimensional vectors. The cross product of two vectors is always a vector (and is never a scalar). So it's also called the vector product.

i. Algebraic
If $\vec{v} = \langle v_1, v_2, v_3 \rangle$ and $\vec{w} = \langle w_1, w_2, w_3 \rangle$, then

$$\vec{v} \times \vec{w} = \langle v_2 w_3 - v_3 w_2, v_3 w_1 - v_1 w_3, v_1 w_2 - v_2 w_1 \rangle.$$

ii. Geometric
The cross product of two vectors is a vector whose length is the product of the two vectors' lengths times the sine of the angle between them. That is,

$$\|\vec{v} \times \vec{w}\| = \|\vec{v}\| \|\vec{w}\| \sin\theta.$$

Also, the direction of the cross product is perpendicular to the two vectors and points in a direction determined by the Right Hand Rule. Using your right hand, point your fingers in the direction of $\vec{v}$. Keeping your fingers pointing that way, rotate your hand until curling your fingers would make them point in the direction of $\vec{w}$. Now your thumb points in the direction of $\vec{v} \times \vec{w}$.

iii. Why is the cross product important?

The cross product provides a vector that is perpendicular to the plane spanned by two given vectors. Physicists use the cross product with vector quantities and vector fields. For example, torque is the cross product of a force vector with a displacement vector on which the force acts. If a force pulls directly away from a point, ($\theta = 0°$) then that point experiences zero torque from that force.

6. Sample Problems

(a) Draw a picture describing $\langle -3, 5 \rangle + \langle 3, -3 \rangle$.

(b) Draw a picture describing $3 \langle -1, 2 \rangle$.

(c) If $\vec{v}$ has magnitude 13 and points in a direction 135° counter-clockwise from the positive x-axis, then find the magnitude and direction of $2\vec{v}$ and $-3\vec{v}$.

(d) Find the magnitude and direction of $\vec{i} + \vec{j}$.

(e) Give an example showing that the two definitions of the dot product are the same.

(f) Give an example showing that the two definitions of the cross product are the same.

(g) (CSET Sample Test #11) Given any two unit vectors $\vec{a}$ and $\vec{b}$, explain why

$$-1 \leq (\vec{a} \cdot \vec{b}) \leq 1.$$

(h) Show on a graph that any vector $\vec{v} = v_1 \vec{i} + v_2 \vec{j}$ which is perpendicular to $2\vec{i} + \vec{j}$ has to satisfy $2v_1 + v_2 = 0$. [Hint: think of slopes.]

7. Answers to Sample Problems

(a) Draw a picture describing $\langle -3, 5 \rangle + \langle 3, -3 \rangle$.

(b) Draw a picture describing $3 \langle -1, 2 \rangle$.

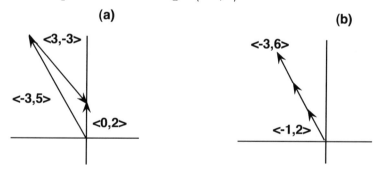

(c) If $\vec{v}$ has magnitude 13 and points in a direction 135° counter-clockwise from the positive x-axis, then find the magnitude and direction of $2\vec{v}$ and $-3\vec{v}$. $2\vec{v}$ has magnitude 26 and points 135° counter-clockwise from the positive x-axis, while $-3\vec{v}$ has magnitude 39, but points 315° counter-clockwise (or 45° clockwise) from the positive x-axis.

(d) Find the magnitude and direction of $\vec{i} + \vec{j}$. The magnitude is $\sqrt{2}$ and the direction is 45° counterclockwise from the positive x-axis.

(e) Give an example showing that the two definitions of the dot product are the same. There are many answers. Consider the example $\langle -1, 1 \rangle \cdot \langle 2, 0 \rangle$. Algebraically, the dot product is $(-1)(2) + (1)(0) = -2$. Geometrically, the magnitude of the first vector is $\sqrt{2}$ and the magnitude of the second vector is 2. The angle between them is $135°$. So the geometric version of the dot product is

$$(\sqrt{2})(2)(\cos 135°) = 2\sqrt{2}\left(-\frac{\sqrt{2}}{2}\right) = -2.$$

(f) Give an example showing that the two definitions of the cross product are the same. There are many answers. Consider the example $\langle 1, 1, 0 \rangle \times \langle 1, 0, 0 \rangle$. There is a $45°$ angle between these vectors. Algebraically, the cross product is $0\vec{i} + 0\vec{j} + (-1)\vec{k} = -\vec{k}$. Geometrically, the magnitude of the cross product is $(\sqrt{2})(1)(\sin 45°) = \sqrt{2}(\frac{\sqrt{2}}{2}) = 1$ and the direction is perpendicular to the xy-plane, in a direction given by the Right Hand Rule. Thus the geometric version of the cross product gives $-\vec{k}$ as well.

(g) (CSET Sample Test #11) Given any two unit vectors $\vec{a}$ and $\vec{b}$, explain why

$$-1 \le (\vec{a} \cdot \vec{b}) \le 1.$$

From the geometric version of the dot product, we know that

$$\vec{a} \cdot \vec{b} = \|\vec{a}\|\|\vec{b}\| \cos \theta,$$

where θ is the angle between $\vec{a}$ and $\vec{b}$. Since $\vec{a}$ and $\vec{b}$ are unit vectors, their magnitudes equal 1. So $\vec{a} \cdot \vec{b} = \cos \theta$, which is always between -1 and 1.

(h) Show on a graph that any vector $\vec{v} = v_1\vec{i} + v_2\vec{j}$ which is perpendicular to $2\vec{i} + \vec{j}$ has to satisfy $2v_1 + v_2 = 0$. [Hint: think of slopes.]

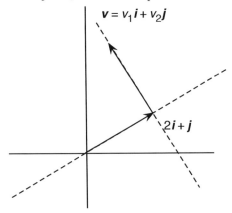

Notice that the slope of any vector $a\vec{i} + b\vec{j}$ is $\frac{\text{rise}}{\text{run}} = \frac{b}{a}$. So the slope of $2\vec{i} + \vec{j}$ is $\frac{1}{2}$. Since perpendicular lines have negative reciprocal slopes, the slope of $\vec{v}$ must be -2. So

$$-2 = \frac{v_2}{v_1} \Rightarrow -2v_1 = v_2 \Rightarrow 0 = 2v_1 + v_2.$$

b. Prove the basic properties of vectors (e.g., perpendicular vectors have zero dot product)

1. What are some basic properties of vectors?

   (a) Assume $\vec{v} \neq \vec{0} \neq \vec{w}$. Then $\vec{v} \cdot \vec{w} = 0$ if and only if $\vec{v} \perp \vec{w}$.

   Proof: From the geometric definition of the dot product (above),

   $$\vec{v} \cdot \vec{w} = \|\vec{v}\| \|\vec{w}\| \cos\theta,$$

   where θ is the angle between $\vec{v}$ and $\vec{w}$. Since the vectors have nonzero lengths, this dot product equals zero if and only if $\cos\theta = 0$. But this means $\theta = 90°$; that is, $\vec{v} \perp \vec{w}$.

   (b) Assume $\vec{v} \neq \vec{0} \neq \vec{w}$. Then $\vec{v} \times \vec{w} = \vec{0}$ if and only if $\vec{v}$ and $\vec{w}$ are parallel or anti-parallel.

   Proof: From the geometric definition of the cross product (above),

   $$\|\vec{v} \times \vec{w}\| = \|\vec{v}\| \|\vec{w}\| \sin\theta,$$

   where θ is the angle between $\vec{v}$ and $\vec{w}$. Since the vectors have nonzero lengths, this dot product equals zero if and only if $\sin\theta = 0$. But this means that either $\theta = 0°$, in which case $\vec{v}$ is parallel to $\vec{w}$, or that $\theta = 180°$, in which case $\vec{v}$ is anti-parallel to $\vec{w}$.

2. Sample Problems

   (a) Let $\vec{v} = 2\vec{i} - 3\vec{j}$ and let $\vec{w} = 7\vec{i} + \vec{j} - 3\vec{k}$. Find the following.

       i. $\vec{v} \cdot \vec{w}$

       ii. $\vec{v} \times \vec{w}$

       iii. $\|\vec{v}\|$ and $\|\vec{w}\|$

       iv. the angle between $\vec{v}$ and $\vec{w}$

   (b) Using the example above, show that $\vec{v} \times \vec{w}$ is perpendicular to $\vec{v}$ and to $\vec{w}$.

   (c) Show that $\vec{v} \times \vec{w}$ is always perpendicular to $\vec{v}$ and to $\vec{w}$.

   (d) Show that $(\vec{v} \times \vec{w}) = -(\vec{w} \times \vec{v})$.

   (e) Show that $\vec{u} \cdot (\vec{v} + \vec{w}) = \vec{u} \cdot \vec{v} + \vec{u} \cdot \vec{w}$. You can assume $\vec{u}$, $\vec{v}$, and $\vec{w}$ are two-dimensional. [The property is true in general.]

   (f) Show that $(\alpha\vec{v}) \cdot \vec{w} = \vec{v} \cdot (\alpha\vec{w}) = \alpha(\vec{v} \cdot \vec{w})$, where α is a scalar (real number). You can assume $\vec{v}$ and $\vec{w}$ are two-dimensional. [The property is true in general.]

   (g) Using the Law of Cosines [In $\triangle ABC$, $c^2 = a^2 + b^2 - 2ab\cos C$.], derive the geometric definition of the dot product. [Hint: draw a triangle of sides $\vec{v}$, $\vec{w}$, and $\vec{w} - \vec{v}$ and apply the formula for length: $\vec{v} \cdot \vec{v} = \|\vec{v}\|^2$.]

3. Answers to Sample Problems

   (a) Let $\vec{v} = 2\vec{i} - 3\vec{j}$ and let $\vec{w} = 7\vec{i} + \vec{j} - 3\vec{k}$. Find the following.

       i. $\vec{v} \cdot \vec{w} = 11$

       ii. $\vec{v} \times \vec{w} = 9\vec{i} + 6\vec{j} + 23\vec{k}$

iii. $\|\vec{v}\| = \sqrt{13}$ and $\|\vec{w}\| = \sqrt{59}$

iv. the angle between $\vec{v}$ and $\vec{w}$ is $\arccos\left(\dfrac{11}{\sqrt{767}}\right) \approx 1.16$ radians, or $66.6°$.

(b) Using the example above, show that $\vec{v} \times \vec{w}$ is perpendicular to $\vec{v}$ and to $\vec{w}$. Using the dot product, $\vec{v} \cdot (\vec{v} \times \vec{w}) = 2(9) + (-3)(6) = 18 - 18 = 0$. Similarly, $\vec{w} \cdot (\vec{v} \times \vec{w}) = 7(9) + 1(6) - 3(23) = 63 + 6 - 69 = 0$.

(c) Show that $\vec{v} \times \vec{w}$ is always perpendicular to $\vec{v}$ and to $\vec{w}$. We will show one directly and leave the other part to the reader.

$$
\begin{aligned}
\vec{v} \cdot (\vec{v} \times \vec{w}) &= \langle v_1, v_2, v_3 \rangle \cdot \langle v_2 w_3 - v_3 w_2, \, v_3 w_1 - v_1 w_3, \, v_1 w_2 - v_2 w_1 \rangle \\
&= v_1(v_2 w_3 - v_3 w_2) + v_2(v_3 w_1 - v_1 w_3) + v_3(v_1 w_2 - v_2 w_1) \\
&= v_1 v_2 w_3 - v_1 v_3 w_2 + v_2 v_3 w_1 - v_1 v_2 w_3 + v_1 v_3 w_2 - v_2 v_3 w_1 \\
&= 0 + 0 + 0 = 0.
\end{aligned}
$$

Hence, $\vec{v}$ is perpendicular to $\vec{v} \times \vec{w}$. The proof that $\vec{w}$ is perpendicular to $\vec{v} \times \vec{w}$ is similar.

(d) Show that $(\vec{v} \times \vec{w}) = -(\vec{w} \times \vec{v})$.

$$
\begin{aligned}
\vec{v} \times \vec{w} &= \langle v_2 w_3 - v_3 w_2, \, v_3 w_1 - v_1 w_3, \, v_1 w_2 - v_2 w_1 \rangle \\
&= \langle -(w_2 v_3 - w_3 v_2), \, -(w_3 v_1 - w_1 v_3), \, -(w_1 v_2 - w_2 v_1) \rangle \\
&= -\langle w_2 v_3 - w_3 v_2, \, w_3 v_1 - w_1 v_3, \, w_1 v_2 - w_2 v_1 \rangle = -(\vec{w} \times \vec{v}).
\end{aligned}
$$

(e) Show that $\vec{u} \cdot (\vec{v} + \vec{w}) = \vec{u} \cdot \vec{v} + \vec{u} \cdot \vec{w}$. You can assume $\vec{u}$, $\vec{v}$, and $\vec{w}$ are two-dimensional. [The property is true in general.]

Let $\vec{u} = \langle u_1, u_2 \rangle$, $\vec{v} = \langle v_1, v_2 \rangle$, and $\vec{w} = \langle w_1, w_2 \rangle$. Then $\vec{v} + \vec{w} = \langle v_1 + w_1, v_2 + w_2 \rangle$. So,

$$
\begin{aligned}
\vec{u} \cdot (\vec{v} + \vec{w}) &= u_1(v_1 + w_1) + u_2(v_2 + w_2) \\
&= u_1 v_1 + u_1 w_1 + u_2 v_2 + u_2 w_2 \\
&= (u_1 v_1 + u_2 v_2) + (u_1 w_1 + u_2 w_2) \\
&= \vec{u} \cdot \vec{v} + \vec{u} \cdot \vec{w}.
\end{aligned}
$$

(f) Show that $(\alpha \vec{v}) \cdot \vec{w} = \vec{v} \cdot (\alpha \vec{w}) = \alpha(\vec{v} \cdot \vec{w})$, where α is a scalar (real number). You can assume $\vec{v}$ and $\vec{w}$ are two-dimensional. [The property is true in general.]

Let $\vec{v} = \langle v_1, v_2 \rangle$ and $\vec{w} = \langle w_1, w_2 \rangle$. Then $\alpha\vec{v} = \langle \alpha v_1, \alpha v_2 \rangle$.

$$
\begin{aligned}
(\alpha\vec{v}) \cdot \vec{w} &= (\alpha v_1) w_1 + (\alpha v_2) w_2 \\
&= \alpha(v_1 w_1 + v_2 w_2) = \alpha(\vec{v} \cdot \vec{w}) \\
&= v_1(\alpha w_1) + v_2(\alpha w_2) = \vec{v} \cdot (\alpha\vec{w}).
\end{aligned}
$$

(g) Using the Law of Cosines [In $\triangle ABC$, $c^2 = a^2 + b^2 - 2ab\cos C$.], derive the geometric definition of the dot product. [Hint: draw a triangle of sides $\vec{v}$, $\vec{w}$, and $\vec{w} - \vec{v}$ and apply the formula for length: $\vec{v} \cdot \vec{v} = \|\vec{v}\|^2$.]

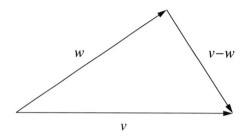

We'll begin with computing the length of the side $\vec{v} - \vec{w}$:

$$
\begin{aligned}
\|\vec{v} - \vec{w}\|^2 &= (\vec{v} - \vec{w}) \cdot (\vec{v} - \vec{w}) \\
&= \vec{v} \cdot \vec{v} - 2\vec{v} \cdot \vec{w} + \vec{w} \cdot \vec{w} \\
&= \|\vec{v}\|^2 + \|\vec{w}\|^2 - 2\vec{v} \cdot \vec{w}.
\end{aligned}
$$

Comparing this to the Law of Cosines, we see that the squares of the side lengths match up, giving $c^2 = a^2 + b^2 - 2\vec{v} \cdot \vec{w}$. Thus

$$-2ab\cos C = -2\vec{v} \cdot \vec{w},$$

which means $\vec{v} \cdot \vec{w} = ab\cos C = \|\vec{v}\|\|\vec{w}\|\cos C$, which is what we wanted. $\square$

c. Understand and apply the basic properties and operations of matrices and determinants (e.g., to determine the solvability of linear systems of equations)

1. What is a matrix?

   A matrix is a rectangular array of numbers. Matrices can be very useful in solving systems of linear equations, among other applications.

2. How do you multiply matrices?

   You can multiply two matrices if the number of columns of the first matrix equals the number of rows of the second matrix. As an example,

   $$
   \begin{bmatrix} a & b \\ c & d \end{bmatrix}
   \begin{bmatrix} 1 & 2 & 3 \\ 4 & 5 & 6 \end{bmatrix}
   =
   \begin{bmatrix} a + 4b & 2a + 5b & 3a + 6b \\ c + 4d & 2c + 5d & 3c + 6d \end{bmatrix}.
   $$

   In general, if A is an m by n matrix and B is an n by p matrix, then AB is an m by p matrix and the entry of AB in row i and column j is given by:

   $$(AB)_{ij} = \sum_{k=1}^{n} A_{ik} B_{kj}.$$

3. What is the determinant of a matrix?

   The determinant of a square matrix is a specific number that encodes some of the properties of that matrix. For instance, if $\det M = 0$, then the matrix M is not invertible. If $\det M \neq 0$, then there is a matrix N satisfying $MN = NM = I$, where I means the identity matrix (1s on the diagonal, 0s elsewhere). In this case, N is also called M^{-1}, the inverse matrix of M.

For 2 by 2 matrices, the determinant is given by:

$$\det \begin{bmatrix} a & b \\ c & d \end{bmatrix} = \begin{vmatrix} a & b \\ c & d \end{vmatrix} = ad - bc.$$

Also, for 2 by 2 matrices, there is a relatively simple formula for finding the inverse matrix:

$$\begin{bmatrix} a & b \\ c & d \end{bmatrix}^{-1} = \left(\frac{1}{ad - bc} \right) \begin{bmatrix} d & -b \\ -c & a \end{bmatrix}, \text{ if } ad - bc \neq 0.$$

For 3 by 3 matrices, the determinant is given by:

$$\begin{vmatrix} a & b & c \\ d & e & f \\ g & h & i \end{vmatrix} = aei + bfg + cdh - bdi - afh - ceg.$$

One way to remember this formula involves recopying the first two columns and then looking along the diagonals of the resulting array.

$$\begin{array}{ccc|cc} a & b & c & a & b \\ d & e & f & d & e \\ g & h & i & g & h \end{array}$$

Multiplying along diagonals down and to the right, we get the terms aei, bfg, and cdh. These are the first three (positive) terms in the determinant formula. Multiplying down and to the left, we obtain the terms bdi, afh, and ceg, which are the next three (negative) terms in the determinant formula.

There is also a recursive way to find the determinant, called expansion by minors. This means that the determinant of a 3 by 3 matrix (for instance) can be written in terms of determinants of various 2 by 2 submatrices of the original matrix. The tricky part is that there is a factor of $(-1)^{r+c}$, where r is the row number and c the column number, counted from the upper left. We'll expand along the top row, although any row or column would work. Pick the first element, a, and then form a submatrix by deleting the row and column containing a. Continue throughout the row. See the example, below.

$$\begin{vmatrix} a & b & c \\ d & e & f \\ g & h & i \end{vmatrix} = (-1)^2 a \begin{vmatrix} e & f \\ h & i \end{vmatrix} + (-1)^3 b \begin{vmatrix} d & f \\ g & i \end{vmatrix} + (-1)^4 c \begin{vmatrix} d & e \\ g & h \end{vmatrix}$$

$$= a(ei - fh) - b(di - fg) + c(dh - eg)$$

$$= aei + bfg + cdh - afh - bdi - ceg.$$

Expansion by minors applies to larger matrices, whereas the trick of repeating the first two columns works only for 3 by 3 matrices.

4. How can you use a matrix to determine the solvability of a system of linear equations?

If you have a system of n linear equations in n variables, you can write it as $A\vec{x} = \vec{b}$, where A is the square (n by n) coefficient matrix, $\vec{x}$ is the vector of variables, and $\vec{b}$ is a column vector of right-hand sides to the equations. See Example, below. Method 1 uses row operations, which are really just manipulations of entire equations. For instance, you can multiply an equation by a constant. So, one valid row operation is to multiply the entire row by a constant.

If A is invertible (that is, if $\det A \neq 0$), then there is exactly one solution to the system, namely $\vec{x} = A^{-1}\vec{b}$. Again, see Example, below, Method 2.

If A is not invertible, then the situation is a little trickier. There might be no solutions (in which case the system of equations is *inconsistent*), or there might be an infinite number of solutions. An example of an inconsistent system is $x + y = 1; x + y = 2$. Clearly these two equations cannot simultaneously be true. An example of a system having an infinite number of solutions is $x + y = 1; 2x + 2y = 2$. This system has an entire line of solution points.

5. How can you use a matrix to solve a system of linear equations?

Example: Solve the equations $2x + 3y = 5$ and $x - y = 5$ simultaneously.

Method 1 (row operations):

$$\begin{bmatrix} 2 & 3 & 5 \\ 1 & -1 & 5 \end{bmatrix} \sim \begin{bmatrix} 1 & -1 & 5 \\ 2 & 3 & 5 \end{bmatrix} \text{ (switch rows)}$$

$$\sim \begin{bmatrix} 1 & -1 & 5 \\ 0 & 5 & -5 \end{bmatrix} \text{ (add } -2(\text{row 1}) \text{ to row 2)}$$

$$\sim \begin{bmatrix} 1 & -1 & 5 \\ 0 & 1 & -1 \end{bmatrix} \text{ (divide row 2 by 5)}$$

So the equations now read $x - y = 5$ and $y = -1$. We can substitute to find that $x = 4$.

Method 2 (inverse matrices): First, rewrite the system of equations in matrix form:

$$\begin{bmatrix} 2 & 3 \\ 1 & -1 \end{bmatrix} \begin{bmatrix} x \\ y \end{bmatrix} = \begin{bmatrix} 5 \\ 5 \end{bmatrix}.$$

Using the formula for the inverse of a 2 by 2 matrix gives:

$$\begin{bmatrix} 2 & 3 \\ 1 & -1 \end{bmatrix}^{-1} = \left(\frac{1}{(2)(-1) - (3)(1)} \right) \begin{bmatrix} -1 & -3 \\ -1 & 2 \end{bmatrix} = \begin{bmatrix} 1/5 & 3/5 \\ 1/5 & -2/5 \end{bmatrix}.$$

So, we can multiply the original matrix equation on the left to obtain:

$$\begin{bmatrix} 1/5 & 3/5 \\ 1/5 & -2/5 \end{bmatrix} \begin{bmatrix} 2 & 3 \\ 1 & -1 \end{bmatrix} \begin{bmatrix} x \\ y \end{bmatrix} = \begin{bmatrix} 1/5 & 3/5 \\ 1/5 & -2/5 \end{bmatrix} \begin{bmatrix} 5 \\ 5 \end{bmatrix},$$

which simplifies to

$$\begin{bmatrix} 1 & 0 \\ 0 & 1 \end{bmatrix} \begin{bmatrix} x \\ y \end{bmatrix} = \begin{bmatrix} x \\ y \end{bmatrix} = \begin{bmatrix} 4 \\ -1 \end{bmatrix}.$$

Therefore, $(x, y) = (4, -1)$.

6. Sample Problems

   (a) Check the formula for the 2 by 2 inverse matrix by calculating AA^{-1} and $A^{-1}A$.

   (b) Give an example of 2 by 2 matrices A and B satisfying $AB \neq BA$.

   (c) Solve the following system of equations: $4x - 3y = 15$ and $6x + y = 6$.

   (d) Solve the following system of equations: $x - y = 12$ and $-3x + 3y = 3$.

   (e) Describe how to solve the following system and set up the appropriate matrix equation, but do not actually solve the system.

   $$
   \begin{aligned}
   34x - 56y + 223z &= 217 \\
   24x + 25y - 100z &= 27 \\
   -30x + 29y + 231z &= -429
   \end{aligned}
   $$

   (f) Find the determinant of $\begin{bmatrix} 11 & 6 \\ 2 & -5 \end{bmatrix}$.

   (g) Find the determinant of $\begin{bmatrix} 4 & 3 & 7 \\ 5 & -5 & 4 \\ 0 & -9 & -8 \end{bmatrix}$.

   (h) Find B so that $AB = C$, where $A = \begin{bmatrix} 3 & 5 \\ -3 & 4 \end{bmatrix}$ and $C = \begin{bmatrix} 9 \\ 9 \end{bmatrix}$.

   (i) Using A and C above, find AC, if possible. Then find CA, if possible.

7. Answers to Sample Problems

   (a) Check the formula for the 2 by 2 inverse matrix by calculating AA^{-1} and $A^{-1}A$. We assume $ad - bc \neq 0$ so that the inverse of A is defined.

   $$
   \begin{bmatrix} a & b \\ c & d \end{bmatrix} \left(\frac{1}{ad - bc} \begin{bmatrix} d & -b \\ -c & a \end{bmatrix} \right) = \frac{1}{ad - bc} \begin{bmatrix} ad - bc & -ab + ba \\ cd - dc & -cb + da \end{bmatrix} = \begin{bmatrix} 1 & 0 \\ 0 & 1 \end{bmatrix},
   $$

   $$
   \left(\frac{1}{ad - bc} \begin{bmatrix} d & -b \\ -c & a \end{bmatrix} \right) \begin{bmatrix} a & b \\ c & d \end{bmatrix} = \frac{1}{ad - bc} \begin{bmatrix} ad - bc & db - bd \\ -ca + ac & -bc + ad \end{bmatrix} = \begin{bmatrix} 1 & 0 \\ 0 & 1 \end{bmatrix}.
   $$

   (b) Give an example of 2 by 2 matrices A and B satisfying $AB \neq BA$. There are many answers.

   $$
   \begin{bmatrix} 0 & 1 \\ 0 & 0 \end{bmatrix} \begin{bmatrix} 0 & 0 \\ 1 & 0 \end{bmatrix} = \begin{bmatrix} 1 & 0 \\ 0 & 0 \end{bmatrix}, \text{ but } \begin{bmatrix} 0 & 0 \\ 1 & 0 \end{bmatrix} \begin{bmatrix} 0 & 1 \\ 0 & 0 \end{bmatrix} = \begin{bmatrix} 0 & 0 \\ 0 & 1 \end{bmatrix}.
   $$

   (c) Solve the following system of equations: $4x - 3y = 15$ and $6x + y = 6$.

   Using matrices, we get

   $$
   \begin{bmatrix} 4 & -3 \\ 6 & 1 \end{bmatrix} \begin{bmatrix} x \\ y \end{bmatrix} = \begin{bmatrix} 15 \\ 6 \end{bmatrix}.
   $$

The inverse of the coefficient matrix is $\dfrac{1}{22}\begin{bmatrix} 1 & 3 \\ -6 & 4 \end{bmatrix}$. So, multiplying both sides (on the left) by this inverse matrix gives:

$$\frac{1}{22}\begin{bmatrix} 1 & 3 \\ -6 & 4 \end{bmatrix}\begin{bmatrix} 4 & -3 \\ 6 & 1 \end{bmatrix}\begin{bmatrix} x \\ y \end{bmatrix} = \frac{1}{22}\begin{bmatrix} 1 & 3 \\ -6 & 4 \end{bmatrix}\begin{bmatrix} 15 \\ 6 \end{bmatrix} = \frac{1}{22}\begin{bmatrix} 33 \\ -66 \end{bmatrix} = \begin{bmatrix} 1.5 \\ -3 \end{bmatrix}.$$

So $x = 1.5$ and $y = -3$.

(d) Solve the following system of equations: $x - y = 12$ and $-3x + 3y = 3$.

Dividing the second equation by -3 gives $x - y = -1$. Hence there are no solutions to this system of equations. The system is inconsistent.

(e) Describe how to solve the following system and set up the appropriate matrix equation, but do not actually solve the system.

$$\begin{aligned} 34x - 56y + 223z &= 217 \\ 24x + 25y - 100z &= 27 \\ -30x + 29y + 231z &= -429 \end{aligned}$$

We can set up a matrix equation and then use row operations or finding an inverse matrix to reduce and solve the system. The corresponding matrix equation is:

$$\begin{bmatrix} 34 & -56 & 223 \\ 24 & 25 & -100 \\ -30 & 29 & 231 \end{bmatrix}\begin{bmatrix} x \\ y \\ z \end{bmatrix} = \begin{bmatrix} 217 \\ 27 \\ -429 \end{bmatrix}.$$

(f) Find the determinant of $\begin{bmatrix} 11 & 6 \\ 2 & -5 \end{bmatrix}$. -67

(g) Find the determinant of $\begin{bmatrix} 4 & 3 & 7 \\ 5 & -5 & 4 \\ 0 & -9 & -8 \end{bmatrix}$. 109

(h) Find B so that $AB = C$, where $A = \begin{bmatrix} 3 & 5 \\ -3 & 4 \end{bmatrix}$ and $C = \begin{bmatrix} 9 \\ 9 \end{bmatrix}$. In order for AB to be a 2 by 1 matrix, we need B to be a 2 by 1 matrix. Let $B = \begin{bmatrix} x \\ y \end{bmatrix}$ and solve. Or, find A^{-1}. Then $B = A^{-1}C$. In any case,

$$B = \begin{bmatrix} -\frac{1}{3} \\ 2 \end{bmatrix}.$$

(i) Using A and C above, find AC, if possible. Then find CA, if possible. $AC = \begin{bmatrix} 72 \\ 9 \end{bmatrix}$. The product CA is not defined because C has only one column, but A has two rows.

d. Analyze the properties of proportional relationships, lines, linear equations, and their graphs, and the connections between them

1. What are some properties of proportional relationships and their graphs?

   (a) What is a proportional relationship?

   (In what follows, we revisit and expand on what was covered in section **1.1.d** on proportional relationships.)

   A proportional relationship can be described in a number of equivalent ways. One way is to describe it in terms of an equation. We say that A is proportional to B if there is some constant k satisfying $A = kB$. The number k is called the "constant of proportionality."

   Another equivalent way to describe a proportional relationship is to say that two quantities are in proportion if every time one quantity is increased by a certain constant amount, then the other quantity is also increased by another constant (possibly different) amount.

   A third way to describe it is to say that two quantities are in proportion if whenever one quantity is multiplied by a certain number, then the other quantity will also be multiplied by the same number.

   We will use the equation formulation most of the time, but there is understanding to be gained when students can switch back and forth between these representations.

   (b) What does the graph of a proportional relationship look like?

   If A is proportional to B, then we can graph that by putting A on the y-axis and B on the x-axis. The graph of $A = kB$ is a straight line that passes through the origin. The slope of this line is k. Slope was introduced in section **2.3.b**.

   (c) What are the important features of a proportional relationship, and how do they relate to its graph?

   We have touched on the important features a little bit when we talked about the different equivalent ways of describing a proportional relationship. Each of these relate to a graph of a straight line passing through the origin, and can be explained using similar triangles. For example, if we add a certain amount to the x-coordinate, then the y-coordinate will change by a constant amount that is exactly k times the change in x. In the first picture below, k is equal to 3.

   Also, if we multiply the x-coordinate by a constant, then the y-coordinate will be multiplied by the same constant. In the second picture below, we have doubled the x-coordinate.

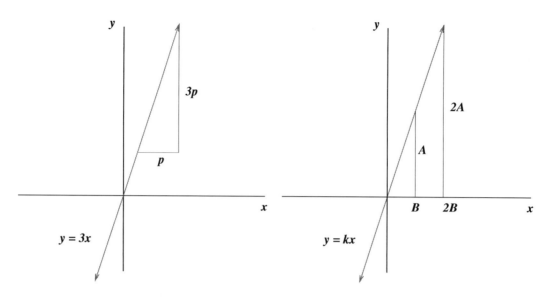

(d) What are some different kinds of proportional relationships?

I like to explain to my students that "is proportional to" means "equals a constant times". So, A is proportional to B means A equals a constant times B, or $A = kB$.

This can be expanded to sentences like A is proportional to the square of B. So $A = kB^2$. Graphing this on a set of axes of A versus B will no longer yield a straight line, but if we were to graph A versus B^2, then we would see a straight line again.

There is also a phrase "is inversely proportional to", which means "is proportional to the reciprocal of". So if A is inversely proportional to B, then A is proportional to the reciprocal of B, or $A = \dfrac{k}{B}$.

These can also be combined in statements like: A is proportional to the cube of B and inversely proportional to the square root of C. Thus $A = \dfrac{kB^3}{\sqrt{C}}$.

Again, only when comparing two quantities that are (directly) proportional does one obtain a graph that is a straight line passing through the origin.

(e) What are some examples of proportional relationships?

Example 1: Suppose you buy food in bulk. The price you pay for dried lentils is proportional to their weight. Suppose that 1.5 pounds of lentils costs \$1.20. Find the constant of proportionality and interpret it in terms of the problem.

We are given that the price is proportional to the weight. Let's keep the units on these quantities, which will allow us to determine the units on k. So,

$$1.2 \text{ dollars} = k(1.5 \text{ pounds}) \implies k = \frac{1.2 \text{ dollars}}{1.5 \text{ pounds}} = 0.8 \text{ dollars per pound.}$$

So k is the price of lentils per pound.

Example 2: When you are driving at a constant speed, say 70 miles per hour, then the distance traveled is proportional to the time that you have been driving. Find a model for this situation.

Here, we are not given any specific quantities, but we are told that we are driving at a rate of 70 miles per hour. So that means that if we drive for one hour, we would have traveled 70 miles. So, 70 miles $= k(1$ hour$)$. Thus $k = 70$ miles per hour. The constant of proportionality is exactly the constant driving speed. To put it in language that is similar to what is taught in Calculus, k is the rate of change of our distance traveled with respect to time.

This is generally true when modeling a proportion problem. If A is proportional to B, and $A = kB$, then k is the (constant) rate of change of A with respect to B.

2. What are some properties of linear equations and their graphs?

See section **2.3.b** for information about linear functions, lines, and their graphs.

3. What are some connections between proportional relationships, linear equations, and their graphs?

The straight line is the graphical connection between all of these. Proportional relationships are graphed as straight lines that go through the origin. We should point out that they do not include vertical lines through the origin. They all have the property that if you multiply one of the quantities by a constant, then the other quantity will get multiplied by that same constant.

Linear equations, on the other hand, also have straight lines as graphs, but they can include vertical lines, and they can include lines that do not pass through the origin. They do not necessarily have the property that multiplying one quantity by a constant will cause the other quantity to be multiplied by the same constant, but they do share the following property with proportional relationships: that if you add a constant amount to one quantity, then the other quantity will be increased by a constant multiple of the increase to the first quantity. And this constant multiple is the same no matter what increase you start with. This constant even has a special name: either the "constant of proportionality" or the "slope."

Another way to think of it is that all proportional relationships can be graphed as lines with a defined slope, but not all linear equations describe proportional relationships.

4. Sample Problems

   (a) Determine if each of the following situations describes a proportional relationship or not.

      i. The cost of buying socks is related to the number of pairs of socks you buy.

      ii. The cost of cable TV is related to the number of channels you order.

      iii. The amount you pay to the doctor is related to the number of visits you make. (Assume you have a health plan.)

   (b) Suppose that the cost of a plane ticket were proportional to the distance traveled. If it costs $770 to fly 1221 miles, then how much would a ticket cost to fly 555 miles?

   (c) TRUE or FALSE: Every linear function f can be thought of as expressing a proportional relationship between the change in x and the change in f. (Explain your answer.)

5. Answers to Sample Problems

(a) Determine if each of the following situations describes a proportional relationship or not.

    i. The cost of buying socks is related to the number of pairs of socks you buy. YES, proportional.

    ii. The cost of cable TV is related to the number of channels you order. NO, not proportional. (Premium channels cost more than others.)

    iii. The amount you pay to the doctor is related to the number of visits you make. (Assume you have a health plan.) NO, not proportional. (If you have a health plan, chances are you have to pay something even if you don't visit the doctor. So the graph would not pass through the origin.)

(b) Suppose that the cost of a plane ticket were proportional to the distance traveled. If it costs \$770 to fly 1221 miles, then how much would a ticket cost to fly 555 miles? \$350.

(c) TRUE or FALSE: Every linear function f can be thought of as expressing a proportional relationship between the change in x and the change in f. (Explain your answer.) TRUE. This is what the slope formula describes. Let $y = f(x)$. Since f is assumed to be a linear function, then we know it has a slope m. We also know that $m = \dfrac{y_2 - y_1}{x_2 - x_1} = \dfrac{\Delta y}{\Delta x}$. This means that $\Delta y = m(\Delta x)$, which describes a proportional relationship. The change in f is proportional to the change in x, and the constant of proportionality is the slope.

e. Model and solve problems using linear equations, pairs of simultaneous linear equations, and their graphs

1. What are some examples of linear models?

   We have already given an example of a linear model in section **2.3.f**. For another example, consider the act of reading a book. The number of pages read in a book depends linearly on the amount of time spent reading. (This assumes that each page has roughly the same number of words on it, is roughly at the same difficulty level, etc.) Suppose that after 40 minutes, you have read 46 pages. How much will you have read after an hour?

   To set up the model, let's use m for the number of minutes spent reading, and p for the number of pages read. This model is strictly proportional - zero pages have been read after zero minutes. So we can write $p = km$, where k is some constant. Using the given information, we get $46 = k(40)$, or $k = \dfrac{46}{40} = \dfrac{23}{20}$. So our model is $p = \dfrac{23}{20}m$.

   To determine how many pages have been read after an hour, we can set $m = 60$. Then

$$p = \frac{23}{20}(60) = (23)(3) = 69.$$

So 69 pages have been read after one hour.

2. How do you solve a system of linear equations?

   In section **c.** above, we saw how to solve a system of linear equations using matrices. We now talk about finding exact and approximate solutions.

- How do you find exact solutions?

  The main methods have been mentioned above: replacing one equation by its sum with a multiple of another equation, replacing one equation by a nonzero multiple of itself, switching the order of equations, and substitution. If a system can be solved exactly, it will usually be by a combination of these approaches.

- How do you find approximate solutions?

  Approximate solutions can be found by graphing, or by using technology, such as a graphing calculator or other mathematical software. Sketching the graphs of the equations that make up the system allows one to see if the individual graphs intersect. The intersection points are the solutions to the system. To use a graphing calculator or other software, consult the manual or online help features.

- What are some examples?

  We'll look at two ways to solve the system the equations: $2x + 3y = 5$ and $x - y = 5$. (Notice that these are the same systems we solved using matrices above.)

  Method 1 (manipulating equations): By looking at the left-hand sides, we see a $3y$ term in the first equation and a $-y$ term in the second equation. So let's add 3 times the second equation to the first equation. This gives

  $$2x + 3y + 3(x - y) = 5 + 3(5) \quad \text{and} \quad x - y = 5 \text{ or:}$$
  $$5x = 20 \quad \text{and} \quad x - y = 5.$$

  From here, we can divide the first equation by 5 (or multiply it by $\frac{1}{5}$). So the equations now read $x = 4$ and $x - y = 5$. We can now substitute to find that $y = -1$. The solution to the system is the single point $(4, -1)$.

  Method 2 (substitution): First, we will rewrite the second equation to solve for x, obtaining $x = y + 5$. We now substitute this expression into the first equation for x to obtain:

  $$2(y + 5) + 3y = 5 \iff 2y + 10 + 3y = 5 \iff 5y = -5.$$

  From here, we can multiply the equation by $\frac{1}{5}$ (or divide by 5) to obtain $y = -1$. Then, since $x = y + 5$, $x = 4$. Therefore, $(x, y) = (4, -1)$ is the solution.

  Next, let's solve the following system of equations: $4x - 3y = 15$ and $6x + y = 6$. As before, let's add 3 times the second equation to the first. This makes the first equation into $4x - 3y + 3(6x + y) = 15 + 3(6)$, or after simplification, $22x = 33$, which means $x = \frac{3}{2} = 1.5$. From here, we can use either equation to determine the value of y. Using the second equation, we get $6(1.5) + y = 6$, or $9 + y = 6$, from which we get $y = -3$. So $x = 1.5$ and $y = -3$.

  Next, let's solve the following system of equations: $x - y = 12$ and $-3x + 3y = 3$. Dividing the second equation by -3 (or multiplying by $-\frac{1}{3}$) gives $x - y = -1$. So our system is now $x - y = 12$ and $x - y = -1$. Hence there are no solutions to this system of equations. Such a system is called *inconsistent*. If we had tried to add 3 times the first equation to the second, we would have obtained $-3x + 3y + 3(x - y) = 3 + 3(12)$, or $0 = 39$, which is clearly not a true statement. That is a sure sign of an inconsistent system.

And as a final example, let's solve the system $x - 5y = 2$ and $-2x + 10y = -4$. Here, let's add 2 times the first equation to the second, to obtain:

$$-2x + 10y + 2(x - 5y) = -4 + 2(2),$$

or $0 = 0$. What does this mean?

It means that the second equation is a multiple of the first. Thus, we really only need one of the equations. This system has an infinite number of solutions, namely any pair (x, y) that satisfies $x - 5y = 2$ will necessarily satisfy the system. Here, the original equations are said to be *dependent* on each other.

3. What are some examples of models involving a pair of simultaneous linear equations?

We will present two examples here, and then will solve them using the techniques we just described.

Example 1: Jane buys three oranges and two apples at the store and pays $1.50. Johnny buys four oranges and three apples at the same store and pays $2.11. How much does each fruit cost?

To solve this, we first need to set up the system of equations. Let's use O for the price of an orange and A for the price of an apple. (Make sure not to confuse the letter O with zero.) Then from what Jane bought, we know $3O + 2A = 1.5$, and from what Johnny bought, we know $4O + 3A = 2.11$. So

$$\begin{aligned} 3O + 2A &= 1.5 \\ 4O + 3A &= 2.11. \end{aligned}$$

Let's multiply the first equation by 3 and the second equation by -2. Then we get

$$\begin{aligned} 9O + 6A &= 4.5 \\ -8O - 6A &= -4.22. \end{aligned}$$

If we now add the two equations (and replace one of them with the sum), we get

$$\begin{aligned} 9O + 6A &= 4.5 \\ O &= 0.28 \end{aligned}$$

So one orange costs $0.28. With this information, we can go back to either initial equation to find that one apple costs $0.33.

Let's check these answers. Three oranges and two apples should cost $3(0.28) + 2(0.33) = 0.84 + 0.66 = 1.5$, while four oranges and three apples cost $4(0.28) + 3(0.33) = 1.12 + 0.99 = 2.11$. So yes, these answers are correct.

Example 2: Suppose you have a solution that is 20% bleach and a solution that is 4% bleach. You need to make 32 ounces of a solution that is 7% bleach. How much of each solution needs to be mixed together to accomplish this?

It may seem like there aren't two equations here. But there are two different amounts in question: the total amount of liquid, and the total amount of bleach in the liquid. We can model this situation with a system of linear equations. Let x be the number of ounces of the 20% bleach solution needed, and let y be the number of ounces of the 4% bleach solution needed. Then, since we need 32 ounces total, we know $x + y = 32$.

Then, since we need 32 ounces of a 7% bleach solution, we know we need $(32)(0.07) = 2.24$ ounces of bleach total. Similarly, the amount of bleach in x ounces of the 20% solution is $(0.2)x$, while the amount of bleach in y ounces of the 4% solution is $(0.04)y$. So, we know that $(0.2)x + (0.04)y = 2.24$.

Before writing the system, we will multiply the second equation by 25. (You can think of multiplying by 100 and then dividing by 4 to reduce.)

$$\begin{aligned} x + y &= 32 \\ 5x + y &= 56 \end{aligned}$$

Using the first equation to solve for y, we get $y = 32 - x$. Substituting into the second equation, we get $5x + (32 - x) = 56$, or $4x = 24$. So $x = 6$. Then $y = 32 - 6 = 26$.

Let's check. Certainly $6 + 26 = 32$ total ounces. To check the bleach, $(0.2)(6) + (0.04)(26) = 1.2 + 1.04 = 2.24$ total ounces of bleach. The answers are correct.

4. Sample Problems

   (a) Find the cost of a pound of beef and a pound of potatoes given the following information. 120 pounds of beef and 315 pounds of potatoes cost \$735 total, while 150 pounds of beef and 420 pounds of potatoes cost \$930 total. (Round to the nearest cent.)

   (b) On Monday, the M&M factory makes candies that are 33% brown, while on Tuesday, they make candies that are 25% brown. How much of each day's candies do they need to mix together to have one ton (2000 pounds) of candies that are 30% brown? (Round to the nearest pound.)

   (c) It takes Jane and Johnny 75 minutes to paint a room in their house. When Johnny's brother helps them, it only takes 55 minutes. Assuming that Johnny and his brother paint at the same rate, find how long it would take Jane to paint the room by herself, and how long it would take Johnny to paint the room by himself. (Round to the nearest minute. Hint: find each one's painting rate.)

5. Answers to Sample Problems

   (a) Find the cost of a pound of beef and a pound of potatoes given the following information. 120 pounds of beef and 315 pounds of potatoes cost \$735 total, while 150 pounds of beef and 420 pounds of potatoes cost \$930 total. (Round to the nearest cent.) Beef costs \$5 per pound, while potatoes cost $\frac{3}{7}$ of a dollar per pound, or about 43 cents per pound.

   (b) On Monday, the M&M factory makes candies that are 33% brown, while on Tuesday, they make candies that are 25% brown. How much of each day's candies do they need to mix together to have one ton (2000 pounds) of candies that are 30% brown? (Round to the nearest pound.) They should mix 1250 pounds of Monday's candies with 750 pounds of Tuesday's candies.

(c) It takes Jane and Johnny 75 minutes to paint a room in their house. When Johnny's brother helps them, it only takes 55 minutes. Assuming that Johnny and his brother paint at the same rate, find how long it would take Jane to paint the room by herself, and how long it would take Johnny to paint the room by himself. (Round to the nearest minute. Hint: find each one's painting rate.) Jane paints at a rate of $\frac{7}{825}$ rooms per minute, while Johnny paints at a rate of $\frac{4}{825}$ rooms per minute. Thus Jane paints a room in $\frac{825}{7} \approx 118$ minutes when working alone, while Johnny paints a room in $\frac{825}{4} \approx 206$ minutes when working alone.

Miscellaneous Extra Review Topics

a. Logarithms

1. What is a logarithm?

   A logarithm is an exponent. The logarithm base b of n is the exponent needed on b to obtain n. In symbols:
   $$x = \log_b n \iff b^x = n.$$
   Any simple logarithmic equation can be transformed into an exponential equation according to the formula above. One consequence of this definition is that you cannot take the logarithm of a number unless that number is positive. This is because basic exponential functions only take positive values.

   Example: Find $\log_3 \frac{1}{81}$.

   Let $x = \log_3 \frac{1}{81}$. Then $3^x = \frac{1}{81} = \frac{1}{3^4} = 3^{-4}$. So, $x = -4$. Therefore, $\log_3 \frac{1}{81} = -4$.

2. What are some bases for logarithms?

   The bases most often used are 10 and e. Logs base 10 are called "common" logs and are written "log" (with no subscript). Logs base e are called "natural" logs and are written "ln."

   Aside: By the way, $e \approx 2.718281828459045\ldots$ One reason e is so useful has to do with calculus. The slope of the graph of $y = e^x$ at any point is equal to the y-coordinate of that point. So, e^x is its own derivative. (See Derivatives, Test 3 materials.)

3. What are some properties of logarithms?

   The following properties hold for any base, b.

   (a) $x = \log_b n \iff b^x = n$ (the definition)

   (b) $\log_b(x^m) = m \log_b x$

   (c) $\log_b(xy) = \log_b x + \log_b y$

   (d) $\log_b x = \dfrac{\log x}{\log b} = \dfrac{\ln x}{\ln b} = \dfrac{\log_a x}{\log_a b}$ (for any base a) [Change of Base Formula]

   The following facts may help you solve log problems.

   (a) $\log_b 1 = 0$. (In particular, $\log 1 = \ln 1 = 0$.)

   (b) $\log_b b = 1$. (In particular, $\log 10 = \ln e = 1$.)

   (c) $\log_b 0$ is not defined.

   (d) $b^{\log_b x} = x$. (In particular, $10^{\log x} = e^{\ln x} = x$.)

   More properties can be found in the Sample Problems.

   Example: Simplify $\log 16 + \log 125 - \log 2$.

Answer: Using the properties, we can deduce that $\log_b \frac{x}{y} = \log_b x - \log_b y$. (See Sample Problems, below.) So, working backwards, we get

$$
\begin{aligned}
\log 16 + \log 125 - \log 2 &= \log \frac{(16)(125)}{(2)} \\
&= \log 1000 \\
&= \log 10^3 \\
&= 3 \log 10 \\
&= 3.
\end{aligned}
$$

4. Sample Problems

   (a) Simplify, if possible:

      i. $\log_4 64$

      ii. $\log_2 128$

      iii. $\log 0.000001$

      iv. $\ln e^{-1}$

      v. $\ln(-e)$

      vi. $\log_7 7$

      vii. $e^{\ln 4}$

      viii. $\log_2 5 - \log_2 40$

      ix. $\log_2 4^t$

      x. $e^{2 \ln w}$

      xi. $\log 10^{4x}$

      xii. $(\log e)(\ln 10)$ [Hint: Use the Change of Base Formula.]

   (b) Write as a single logarithm: $2 \ln w + 5 \ln x - \frac{1}{2} \ln y$.

   (c) Expand as a sum of logarithms of single variables: $\log_5 \left(\dfrac{x^7}{y^2 \sqrt[3]{z}} \right)$.

   (d) Solve for x: $\log_6 x + \log_6(x+5) = 1$.

   (e) Why does $\log_6 x - \log_6(x+5) = 1$ not have a real solution?

   (f) Using the log properties, show that $\log_b b^m = m$.

   (g) Using the log properties, show that $\log_b \frac{x}{y} = \log_b x - \log_b y$.

5. Answers to Sample Problems

   (a) Simplify, if possible:

      i. $\log_4 64 = 3$

      ii. $\log_2 128 = 7$

      iii. $\log 0.000001 = -6$

      iv. $\ln e^{-1} = -1$

v. $\ln(-e)$ is not defined.

vi. $\log_7 7 = 1$

vii. $e^{\ln 4} = 4$

viii. $\log_2 5 - \log_2 40 = \log_2(\frac{1}{8}) = -3$

ix. $\log_2 4^t = \log_2(2^{2t}) = 2t$

x. $e^{2\ln w} = e^{\ln w^2} = w^2$

xi. $\log 10^{4x} = 4x$

xii. $(\log e)(\ln 10) = \left(\dfrac{\ln e}{\ln 10}\right)(\ln 10) = 1$

(b) Write as a single logarithm: $2\ln w + 5\ln x - \frac{1}{2}\ln y$. $\ln\left(\dfrac{w^2 x^5}{\sqrt{y}}\right)$

(c) Expand as a sum of logarithms of single variables: $\log_5\left(\dfrac{x^7}{y^2 \sqrt[3]{z}}\right)$.

$$7\log_5 x - 2\log_5 y - \frac{1}{3}\log_5 z$$

(d) Solve for x: $\log_6 x + \log_6(x+5) = 1$. $x = 1$ ($x = -6$ is extraneous)

$$\log_6 x + \log_6(x+5) = 1 \Rightarrow \log_6(x(x+5)) = 1 \Rightarrow x(x+5) = 6 \Rightarrow$$

$$\Rightarrow x^2 + 5x - 6 = 0 \Rightarrow (x+6)(x-1) = 0 \Rightarrow x = 1 \text{ or } -6$$

Checking both of these shows that -6 is extraneous.

(e) Why does $\log_6 x - \log_6(x+5) = 1$ not have a real solution? If we proceed as in the previous problem, we get $\frac{x}{x+5} = 6$, which has $x = -6$ as a solution. But since $\log_6(-6)$ is not defined, there is no solution to the original equation.

(f) Using the log properties, show that $\log_b b^m = m$. Answers may vary.

$$\log_b b^m = m(\log_b b) = m(1) = m.$$

(g) Using the log properties, show that $\log_b \frac{x}{y} = \log_b x - \log_b y$. Answers may vary.

$$\log_b \frac{x}{y} = \log_b(xy^{-1}) = \log_b x + \log_b(y^{-1}) = \log_b x - \log_b y.$$

b. Proof by Contradiction

1. What is a proof by contradiction?

A proof by contradiction is a way to show that a statement is true by showing that it cannot be false. You assume that it is false, and then show that your assumption leads to a contradiction of some other mathematical fact or hypothesis of the problem.

Aside: This proof technique relies HEAVILY on the "Law of the Excluded Middle," which says that either a mathematical statement is true or else it is false. There is no room for any other outcome.

2. Sample Problems

   (a) Let m be an integer and let m^2 be odd. Then m is odd.

   (b) Let $r, s \in \mathbb{R}$ and let $r + s$ be irrational. Then r is irrational or s is irrational.

   (c) Let m and n be integers and let mn be odd. Then m is odd and n is odd.

   (d) Suppose that n is an integer which is not divisible by 3. Then n is not divisible by 6.

   (e) Prove that $\log_2 3$ is irrational.

3. Answers to Sample Problems

   (a) Let m be an integer and let m^2 be odd. Then m is odd.

   Proof: Suppose that m^2 is odd, but m is even. Then $m = 2k$ for some integer k. So $m^2 = 4k^2 = 2(2k^2)$, which is also even. But this contradicts our hypothesis that m^2 is odd. Therefore m must be odd. $\square$

   (b) Let $r, s \in \mathbb{R}$ and let $r + s$ be irrational. Then r is irrational or s is irrational.

   Proof: Suppose that $r + s$ is irrational, but both r and s are rational. Then there exist integers a, b, c, and d with $b \neq 0 \neq d$ such that $r = \frac{a}{b}$ and $s = \frac{c}{d}$. Then $r + s = \frac{a}{b} + \frac{c}{d} = \frac{ad+bc}{bd}$, which is clearly rational. But this contradicts our hypothesis that $r + s$ is irrational. Therefore r is irrational or s is irrational. $\square$

   (c) Let m and n be integers and let mn be odd. Then m is odd and n is odd.

   Proof: Suppose that mn is odd, but either m or n is even. Without loss of generality, say $m = 2k$ for some integer k. Then $mn = 2kn$, which is clearly even. But this contradicts our hypothesis that mn is odd. So therefore m and n must be odd. $\square$

   (d) Suppose that n is an integer which is not divisible by 3. Then n is not divisible by 6.

   Proof: Suppose that n is not divisible by 3, but that n is divisible by 6. Then there exists an integer k satisfying $n = 6k = 3(2k)$. Thus n is also divisible by 3. But this contradicts our hypothesis that n is not divisible by 3. Therefore, n must not be divisible by 6. $\square$

   (e) Prove that $\log_2 3$ is irrational.

   Proof: Suppose that $\log_2 3$ is rational. Then $\log_2 3 = \frac{p}{q}$ for some integers p and q with $q \neq 0$. Then $2^{p/q} = 3$, or, raising both sides to the q-th power, $2^p = 3^q$. According to the Fundamental Theorem of Arithmetic, the only power of 2 that is also a power of 3 is the number $1 = 2^0 = 3^0$. So $p = q = 0$. But this contradicts the fact that $q \neq 0$. Therefore, $\log_2 3$ must be irrational. $\square$

Made in the USA
San Bernardino, CA
17 May 2017